Schizophrenia

Biological and Psychological
Perspectives

Edited by
GENE USDIN, M.D.
*Clinical Professor of Psychiatry
and Behavioral Sciences
Louisiana State University School of Medicine*

BRUNNER/MAZEL, *Publishers* • NEW YORK

Copyright © 1975 by THE AMERICAN COLLEGE OF PSYCHIATRISTS
Published by
BRUNNER/MAZEL, INC.
64 University Place, New York, N.Y. 10003

All rights reserved, including the right of reproduction
in whole or in part in any form.

MANUFACTURED IN THE UNITED STATES OF AMERICA

Library of Congress Cataloging in Publication Data
Main entry under title:
SCHIZOPHRENIA: BIOLOGICAL AND PSYCHOLOGICAL
    PERSPECTIVES.
    Includes bibliographies.
    1. Schizophrenia. I. Usdin, Gene, 1922-
[DNLM: 1. Schizophrenia—Congresses. WM203 A512s]
RC514.S3347   616.8'982   75-20118
ISBN 0-87630-110-3

CONTRIBUTORS

ROBERT CANCRO, M.D., Med.D.Sc.
Professor of Psychiatry, School of Medicine, University of Connecticut

ARVID CARLSSON, M.D., Ph.D.
Professor of Pharmacology, School of Medicine, University of Goteborg, Sweden

WILLIAM T. CARPENTER, Jr., M.D.
Acting Chief, Psychiatric Assessment Section, Adult Psychiatry Branch, National Institute of Mental Health; Director of Schizophrenia Research Programs, Department of Psychiatry, Bronx Municipal Hospital, Albert Einstein School of Medicine

PAUL CHODOFF, M.D.
Clinical Professor of Psychiatry, School of Medicine, George Washington University

ROY R. GRINKER, Sr., M.D.
Director and Chairman, Institute for Psychosomatic and Psychiatric Research and Training, Michael Reese Hospital and Medical Center; Professor of Psychiatry, Pritzker School of Medicine, University of Chicago

GERALD L. KLERMAN, M.D.
Professor of Psychiatry, Harvard Medical School; Superintendent, Erich Lindemann Mental Health Center

MORRIS A. LIPTON, Ph.D., M.D.
    Director, Biological Sciences Research Center of the Child Development Research Institute; Sarah Graham Kenan Professor of Psychiatry, University of North Carolina Medical School at Chapel Hill

ARNOLD J. MANDELL, M.D.
    Professor and Co-Chairman, Department of Psychiatry, School of Medicine, University of California at San Diego

CONTENTS

Introduction by Gene Usdin, M.D. ix

1. Perspectives in Biology and Psychiatry 1
    Roy R. Grinker, Sr., M.D.

2. Genetic Considerations in the Etiology and
    Prevention of Schizophrenia 16
    Robert Cancro, M.D., Med.D.Sc.

3. The Bucket, the Train, and the Feedback Loop in
    Biochemical Psychiatry 38
    Arnold J. Mandell, M.D.

4. Psychogenic Theories of Schizophrenia 56
    Paul Chodoff, M.D. and
    William T. Carpenter, Jr., M.D.

5. The Clinical Relevance of Recent Research for
    Treatment and Prevention of Schizophrenia ... 80
    Gerald L. Klerman, M.D.

6. Pharmacological Approach to Schizophrenia
    (The Stanley R. Dean Award Lecture) 102
    Arvid Carlsson, M.D., Ph.D.

7. Synthesis: Biological Contributions to the
    Theory and Treatment of Schizophrenia 125
    Morris A. Lipton, Ph.D., M.D.

Introduction

This, the seventh publication of the American College of Psychiatrists, brings to the reader the papers presented at the January, 1975, annual meeting, which was devoted to the topic of schizophrenia. The purpose of this volume is to make available to psychiatrists the current thoughts about schizophrenia which were presented by the speakers to the College members. The American College of Psychiatrists considers its principle *raison d'être* to be postgraduate education of psychiatrists.

Schizophrenia remains a disease whose conceptual framework is fraught with confusion and uncertainty. It has been described as everything from a single disease to an entity transcending the limits of mundane reality. Until such time as we have an independent, valid, definitive test for schizophrenia, all of our efforts to improve reliability of diagnosis will be of limited practicality. The current uncertain state of our knowledge about the description, classification, and etiology of schizophrenia applies to both biologic and psychogenic theories and is a consequence of the lack of diagnostic reliability, the uncertainty as to whether schizophrenia is a single entity, the significant differences between acute and chronic schizophrenia, and the influence of the position of the observer.

A better understanding of the specific gene-environment interactions and their developmental timing will ultimately be useful for control and conservative intervention. A better understanding of those features of development likely to precipitate mental disorder of any type will also be useful for structuring social institutions which can be supportive in nature. The hope for the near future lies in improved treatment and rehabilitation techniques.

This volume begins with the presentation of Roy Grinker, Sr., one of the significant psychiatric statesmen of our time from the viewpoint of administrative, teaching, clinical and research capacities. Grinker provides a brief, personal perspective of the period which has elapsed since he became a physician 50 years ago. He expresses initial discouragement about the slow progress of psychiatry, but then notes the acceleration commencing in the 1950's. He points out that the introduction of drugs has given impetus to a renewed and long-delayed interest in the chemistry of the central nervous system. He notes the many unanswered questions about schizophrenia, but recognizes the various forms of therapy available, with hope for improved prognosis.

Grinker, in common with others throughout the volume, emphasizes the need for continued research and deplores the lack of tangible support for it. He sees psychiatry responding, unfortunately, to many unwise pressures and riding in diverse, often contrary, directions. His presentation terminates with the plea to avoid dichotomies, to recognize that there is no simple answer to many of the problems, and to develop a new direction and a curriculum which would be multidisciplinarian.

Cancro believes that the evidence for the operation of a genetic factor in the etiology of schizophrenia is overwhelming. He decries the resistance to accepting the genetic studies, believing that this opposition is derived from the tendency to look upon environmental and genetic factors as separate sources of influence. It is important to understand that, while the gene-environment distinction is helpful pedagogically, it does not capture the reality of biologic systems. Genetic factors do not operate in the absence of an evoking environment, and environments do not operate in the absence of genetic factors. As an illustration of the arbitrariness of the genetic-environmental distinction, Cancro notes that environmental factors determine which structural genes are enhanced and suppressed. In this very specialized but technically correct sense, one can say that the environment determines the effective genotype. The present-day understanding of behavior genetics is such that we can safely say that, even after establishment of a phenotypic characteristic, there is some openness in the system for alteration and/or correction. Biologic organisms are not fixed. This is simultaneously their great strength and weakness.

Cancro argues for a polygenic model of inheritance involving a small number of genes, and concludes that there is no abnormal gene in schizophrenia but that the traits in question are at the extreme end of a normal distribution curve. Cancro distinguishes between the predisposition or vulnerability to schizophrenia, which is hypothesized as genetically loaded, and the actual environmental experiences and developmental tasks that precipitate the illness. If mental illness in a vulnerable individual decompensates into a psychosis, it will take a schizophrenic form.

An understanding of the role of genetic factors in the etiology of schizophrenia raises a number of questions concerning prevention. It is theoretically and practically possible to reduce the number of vulnerable or predisposed individuals through either genetic or environmental manipulation. But there are implicit dangers in either of these approaches. If we were to be successful in influencing either the genetic pool or the effective genetic repertoire of a given population, we would have done so without advance knowledge of the possible negative consequences. The potential for disaster is sufficiently great that extreme caution is in order. This argument holds even if we are dealing with an "abnormal" gene. If Cancro's model is correct, we would be trying to suppress, through genetic and/or environmental manipulation, the frequency of normal variations in fundamental behavioral traits. If it is in the extreme variation from the midrange of human traits that we find the creative and colorful variance, then we would indeed be paying a high price for a reduction in vulnerability to the disorder.

Mandell's presentation is a provocative, challenging contribution, which utilizes references from the most advanced research in biochemical psychiatry. It does not relate specifically to schizophrenia, but details important concepts of neurotransmitter systems. Mandell notes the shift of emphasis from peripheral metabolites to central synaptic mechanisms with increased attention to the central action of drugs, pointing out that we can actually specify drug-induced neurochemical changes better than we can describe subjective mood alterations. He alerts one to the dangers of the researchers' biases, and points out the two kinds of information forthcoming from endocrinologic research. He decries the assumption that peripheral fluids relate to brain function in a simple and direct way. His concepts of the bucket, the train, and the feedback loop are clever analogies which provide a handle for the reader to grasp in gaining a better understanding of brain functioning. There can be no question, however, that while Mandell's chapter will teach all of us new concepts, it will be heavy reading for those not deeply invested in the field. The author suggests several possible relevant processes in central synapsis of the dopaminergic, noraminergic, and serotonergic systems. Mandell closes by recognizing the possibility that the fragments of neurobiological adaptions being measured today will emerge as prototypic of the mechanisms that serve a variety of brain neurotransmitter systems.

Chodoff and Carpenter provide an overview of the current state of primarily psychogenic theories of schizophrenia, contrasting the current state of retrenchment and even defensiveness about psychogenic theories with the high-water mark reached during the post World War II period. They attribute this present decline in interest to the relative waning of the influence of the psychoanalytic model, the contrast between the apparent efficacy of drug treatment and the uncertain results of psychotherapy, and the fact that a significant genetic factor in some schizophrenia subgroups has been demonstrated beyond reasonable doubt. Of course, genetics are not antithetic to psychological factors—even personality traits have genetic origins. The authors of this paper present a critical summary of psychoanalytic and familial approaches to schizophrenia, describing the present scene as marked by a debate between proponents of an ego deficit and those supporting a conflict theory of origin. Both deficit and conflict models have advantages and disadvantages. An important consequence of espousing one or the other model has to do with its influence on psychotherapeutic approaches, this being more modest in the deficit than in the conflict models (which purport to account for all of the phenomena of schizophrenia on psychogenic grounds). In general, acceptance of a genetic component may have the adverse effect not only of causing therapists to regard schizophrenics as so different, qualitatively, from neurotics as not to be quite human, but also of generating certain kinds of countertransference influences which impede psychotherapy.

Although not ignoring the ways in which psychogenic theories of schizophrenia may be inadequate, Chodoff and Carpenter undertake to defend the usefulness and importance of these theories. They maintain that all schizophrenics, no matter what other factors may be involved in their illnesses, have psychological difficulties which may vary among individuals in degree of severity, but which in no instance can be neglected. Psychogenic research in schizophrenia employs the method of clinical observation, which is the backbone of modern scientific medicine and is not incompatible with the principles of science. They maintain that psychogenic inquiry has developed a reasonable consensus in the following four propositions: 1) Schizophrenia develops out of a family milieu which is seriously, although often subtly, disturbed. 2) This disturbance is marked by faulty and idiosyncratic communicative processes within the family. 3) The early object relationships of the future schizophrenic are seriously stunted. 4) The schizophrenic person is extremely ambivalent in his attitude toward interpersonal closeness. The authors emphasize that psychogenic theories, whatever their limitations, provide an important frame of reference with which to orient the therapist who attempts to enter the chaotic world of the schizophrenic.

Klerman is a strong proponent of the chronic disease model

which, as a variant of the medical model, can be successfully applied to recent research findings in schizophrenia to integrate the available knowledge, to relate the findings to clinical practice, and to develop a public health approach to community mental health and national policy. He states that schizophrenia should be studied by a disease approach because of the intensity, persistence, and degree of interference with the schizophrenic patient's usual psychological, cognitive, and perceptual behavior, and accepted social behaviors.

In spite of critics such as Szasz, who maintains that mental illness is a myth, and Scheff and Rosenhan, who hypothesize that labeling a person as mentally ill is a self-fulfilling prophesy, Klerman constantly emphasizes that schizophrenia best fits the framework of the chronic disease approach of the medical model. Like hypertension, arthritis, and leukemia, schizophrenia represents a symptom complex which, while its boundaries are at times not clearly demarcated, has a certain degree of unity in clinical presentation and characteristic course.

Klerman discusses the application of recent research in schizophrenia to clinical treatment: diagnosis, treatment of the acute episode, lessons from pharmacotherapy, the role of hospitalization, maintenance drug therapy, tardive dyskinesia, the role of the family, and the role of psychotherapy. He discusses the public health concept implication of the recent research emphasis on prevention: primary, secondary, and tertiary (or rehabilitation). The failure of the community mental health centers to incorporate these research findings into treatment practices for schizophrenics remains a severe indictment of this government-sponsored community mental health system.

Klerman believes that the implications of negating the medical model for schizophrenia are a serious challenge to the psychiatric profession and to national health policy, which faces the task of implementing a sociologic model.

Carlsson briefly reviews the history of research on antipsychotic agents for the past 20 years, discussing the various drugs that have been used, the theories of their modus operandi, and the nature of their effect. Throughout his chapter there is an inherent, optimistic feeling that future pharmacologic research will achieve substantial goals in the management of the schizophrenic illnesses.

Carlsson notes that while certain drugs (e.g., the antipsychotic agents) alleviate, others (e.g., the amphetamines) produce or aggravate schizophrenic symptoms. Studies on the mode and site of action of such drugs have yielded important clues. These drugs act on the catecholamines of the brain: whereas the antipsychotic agents inhibit the function of catecholaminergic synapses by either a pre- or postsynaptic action, the amphetamines increase the concentration of these neurohumoral transmitters at receptor sites by inducing release into the synaptic cleft.

Carlsson points out that of the two major brain catecholamines it appears that dopamine is most important in relation to schizophrenia, although the contributory role of norepinephrine cannot be excluded. The evidence supporting these concepts is substantial. For an antipsychotic action, three different mechanisms have been discovered: 1) depletion of transmitter by blocking the storage mechanism of the synaptic vesicles, reserpine being the prototype for this mechanism; 2) blockade of transmitter synthesis by inhibition of the enzyme tyrosine hydroxylase—the agent used here is α-methyltyrosine; and 3) blockade of postsynaptic catecholamine receptors by chlorpromazine, haloperidol, and most of the other currently used antipsychotics. Analyses of the dopamine metabolite homovanillic acid in the cerebrospinal fluid of schizophrenic patients support the view that the actions observed in animals also occur in man. Animal experiments have demonstrated the ability of amphetamines to release catecholamines. Moreover, it has been demonstrated that this release is essential for the central stimulating action. If the animals are pretreated with α-methyltyrosine to inhibit catecholamine synthesis, the stimulating action of amphetamine is blocked. Also, the euphoriant action of amphetamine in man is prevented by α-methyltyrosine.

Carlsson adds that, because of these drug mechanisms, an involvement of catecholamines in schizophrenia might be inferred. However, the essential feature of this disorder might well be an imbalance between different, perhaps mutually antagonistic, systems, one of which is catecholaminergic. If this is so, the primary disturbance may reside either in the catecholaminergic or in the non-catecholaminergic component. Among the candidates worth investigating in the latter case, GABA may be considered. Some recently reported preliminary observations on the clinical effect of a GABA derivative in schizophrenia are of interest in this context.

Lipton, in the final chapter, pulls together the ideas of the other contributors and adds his own research concepts, plus those of certain other researchers which he considers of special consequence. As an eclectic psychiatrist holding a doctorate in pharmacology, Lipton brings a valuable, almost unique, background to the task of synthesizing. He obviously accepts this responsibility with the intention not merely of assimilating the thoughts of others but of being intellectually provocative. He recognizes the advances made in our understanding of schizophrenia, but also sets his sights on future possibilities. As a result, the reader will gain a valuable idea of the directions in which the field is expanding. Lipton closes his report by expressing alarm at the appalling lack of funds available for research in schizophrenia and the poor social climate which now exists with respect to such needs.

All psychiatry is facing a significant crisis today. Indeed, psychiatry's very credibility as a science is being questioned. Therefore, it is the very essence of our professional direction that we continue to learn and grow through such presentations as offered in this book. The potential for each psychiatrist and each professional in the field is inherent in our ability to look at ourselves honestly and to recognize the need to incorporate both research and theory into clinical practice. We can do this only by making a commitment to continuing education and self-exploration.

1

Perspectives in Biology and Psychiatry

Roy R. Grinker, Sr., M.D.

It is difficult to present the historical development of psychiatry from a biological perspective from the time I received my M.D. degree 50 years ago. In summary it has been pitifully slow, frustrating and discouraging, at least up to the 1950's. Yet in the early years of this century physicians did practice psychiatry *and* neurology as so-called neuropsychiatrists, naturally with a strong bias toward organic causations.

What did they do as psychiatrists? In practice they utilized the Kraepelinian classification for diagnosis. Private practitioners treated neuroses by psychotherapies embodying suggestion, support, persuasion and direction, with small doses of sodium bromide. Later they added phenobarbital, although this drug was primarily effective in the treatment of epilepsy. Group, family and behavioral modification therapies were still to come.

The psychoses were the subject of the most boring lectures in the medical curriculum, discouraging to any student interested in psychiatry. Most psychotic patients were sent far from their families, who were presumed to be pathogenic, to private sanitariums, often for a life time. The financially less fortunate were warehoused in state mental hospitals, some for lives of misery and early deaths. The institutions' few psychiatrists spent their time arguing about the diagnosis and prescribing hydrotherapy, sedation or restraint. The psychiatrists had difficulty in understanding the dose variability for different patients of the early pharmacological agents, relying on so-called standard doses.

Some psychiatrists placed their patients in so-called "rest cures," designed according to Weir Mitchell's theories. This included bed-rest and high fat diets to replenish the myelin sheaths. Some neuropsychiatrists hospitalized their patients in general hospitals, using the false diagnosis of suspected brain tumor because there were no psychiatric units. Other patients were placed in hotels with nurses on duty around the clock. Depressions were treated with powdered opium, belladonna and a laxative in capsule form. Another function of the psychiatrists or so-called "alienists" was to testify in court cases involving the sanity of murderers and other criminals.

I received an early important lesson in psychopharmacology from the distinguished internist Frank Billings. Standing in line waiting to enter the University of Chicago's commons for a faculty dinner, he stood in front of me, suddenly turned and breathed in my face. I drew back, and he said, "Young man, I noticed that you pulled away, probably because you smelled alcohol on my breath. Let me tell you now that alcohol is the best antidote to senility."

Many neuropsychiatrists searched for a more basic psychotherapy than suggestion and were ripe for acceptance of psychoanalysis. Others agreed with Kuh (1), who stated in 1911 that psychoanalysis is not a method of observation, but only one of interpretation by means of sophistry. He maintained that it was not theoretically sound, since the *essential conditions for neuroses are constitutional*. Furthermore, on the basis of his own experience, Kuh considered psychoanalysis to be dangerous. Although Freud had warned of transference problems, Kuh said, "... that sort of thing with a hysterical patient is anything but desirable." It was, he noted, an exceedingly serious phase of the method, which had given trouble to a number of men who had used it; besides, the treatment took from six months to three years, and even then the results were doubtful. If one spent as much time and energy with other methods, more would be accomplished with less risk. Finally, Kuh said, psychoanalysis was nothing new; it was only a simple form of suggestion.

On the other hand, my father had stated in a discussion following a lecture by Ernest Jones: "It must be admitted that it is not very easy to understand Freud's viewpoint, and for that reason we are under obligation to the essayist who has in numerous contributions and discussions endeavored to acquaint the American profession with Freud's work. The physician who does not practice psychoanalysis in the broader sense is not competent to treat nervous cases. The man who either had no experience with the method, or else is too indolent to learn it, is a very poor critic indeed and had better learn something about it."

Years afterward when I wanted to be psychoanalysed, my father denounced the field and refused to support my efforts to learn about it, because of his sad experiences with his patients' positive and negative transferences. Twenty-one years later I was analysed by Freud, as my father probably turned over in his grave!

After psychoanalytic training, I began analyzing patients, but this experience only served to teach me significant psychoanalytic theories applicable to psychiatric research and psychotherapy. Then and now, I have not been convinced of the therapeutic successes of psychoanalysis. At any rate I remained within the organization, as a critic, never as a member of the establishment. But I wasted my words, accomplishing little except for my own students (2).

After World War II, we formally established our Institute at Michael Reese in 1946 (3) and planned a new 80-bed hospital for service, research and training, which we occupied in 1951. In the meantime we had established a multidisciplinary team to study the effects of stress (4) on bodily functions (5-10). During the war, Arthur Mirsky had assisted in determining what functions were most disturbed by intense anxiety. This work revealed that liver functions, as measured by hippuric acid excretion, could serve as a marker for the intensity of anxiety (11).

Eventually we recognized that the promised breakthrough by Alexander, attributing specific emotions for the etiology of seven psychosomatic diseases, had failed us (12). We found that general responses to stress stimuli, with or without conscious emotional arousal, without differentiation among the primary affects of anxiety, anger, depression or pleasure, were largely within the pituitary-adrenocortical axis and suggested a preparatory facilitation of stress responders (13). Secondly, we found that there are specific, more or less localized, responses which are individually response-specific. The individual reacts in his personal way when he appraises the dangerous meaning of internal or external stimuli. All this took many years, stirring us to develop a conference on "Unitary Theory of Human Behavior" (14) or "Open Systems sychiatry" (15).

After the discovery of thorazine, although good results were reported at first, our staff prescribed insufficient doses, when they reluctantly prescribed any, and used them for periods of time tooo short to be of use. Now we have antidepressive, antimanic, and antipsychotic drugs. But much still needs to be done to determine timing, intervals and cessation of medication, and specific indications and contraindications. I won't indicate the myriad questions still unanswered. The most important contribution of the work with drugs has been a renewed interest in chemistry of the central nervous system and the specific loci of differences. There has been a long wait since Thudicum!

Thereafter we developed extensive and time consuming clinical investigations. The stress research produced a serendipitous by-product of healthy males (16, 17). We spent six years restudying the phenomena of depressions (18), eight years on the Borderline Syndrome (19) and its four subtypes (non-schizophrenic) and, finally, with Holzman at first (now 10 of us), we have been planning, designing, piloting and actively engaging in studying young adult schizophrenics (20).

Schizophrenia, which we are now studying, is a strange disease, known since antiquity by many names but never thoroughly understood. It exists in all societies and cultures in varying quantities. In fact, schizophrenias are the "cancers" of psychiatry; if anything, they are worse, because some of their manifestations persist throughout life and fatality, unlike that of cancer, occurs most often by suicide (21, 22, 23).

Macfie Campbell (24) stated: "I prefer to think of them as belonging to a Greek letter society, the conditions for admission to which are obscure; inclusion and exclusion from the fraternity are determined by considerations which may vary from year to year and from place to place, and the directing board is not known."

To paraphrase Selye (25): psychiatrists know what schizophrenia is, but they don't know what is schizophrenia. There are at least two reasons for this state of affairs. One is that the manifestations of all psychiatric syndromes have changed over the last several decades (26). We see fewer dramatic, histrionic behaviors but more restricted and constricted characters. Today we see very few fresh catatonic rigidities, immobilities or excitements, and few hebephrenic or childish behaviors indicating almost total regression. Another reason is the fact that individual schizophrenics are highly variable in their feeling, thinking and behavior over the total course of their illness.

Largely because of the variability in individual life histories, cross-sectional studies of the syndrome are inadequate. We need longitudinal studies well past the presumed critical period of the fourth decade of life. Retrospective studies are difficult and hampered by erroneous recall. Prospective studies are time consuming and require frequent follow-up observations, but they are reasonably accurate. For this reason our researches, conducted with Philip Holzman of The University of Chicago Pritzker Medical School, have focused on young first-break schizophrenics who can be followed for approximately two decades.

Personality, character or life style is an expression of the integration of biological, psychological and socio-cultural processes, in other words, a biopsychosocial system. In any so-called disease, some part of this system is awry. This is especially true of schizophrenia, for which investigators have chosen a single part of the system based on their scientific discipline and interest. Of all psychiatric syndromes, schizophrenia best represents a system whose parts range from the biological (biogenetics, biochemistry, etc.) to the socio-cultural (family, group, society, value systems, etc.).

Parts of a system may operate harmoniously in homeostatic cooperation or in opposition in negative feedback processes. One or another part may succumb to stress stimuli or decrease its activities below or increase it beyond its healthy range. Substitution of function and other adaptive mechanisms may successfully hide defects or, in more severe stress responses, disintegration may be augmented.

Theoretically, biological systems are regulated and controlled by some form of organizer. This has been studied carefully in the embryological systems of development where position and timing are important. In psychoanalytic theory the superego concept partially explains the should-nots and shoulds of behavior. In psychoses it seems that either because of internal strains or external stress stimuli, controls are lost or weakened and devolution, dedifferentiation or regression (as synonymous terms) occur to some degree.

The parts of the human system of mentation develop or differentiate from a global state. They become integrated as they differentiate, but are vulnerable to disintegration under adverse circumstances. Interactions of the parts and of the whole with external forces determine the state and degree of health or illness. Although man is not a robot, passively responding to the demands of the environment, he does require environmental stimuli and a modicum of conflict to exist. The ranges of these vary with age and the phenotype or personality derived from the individual's own genetic and experiential history.

Returning to schizophrenia, we have to ask ourselves—as we do for any disease—three questions. These are what, how and why? The *what* is the definition of the disease and its position in a nosological classification; the *how* refers to the multiple causes ending in the disease; and the *why* is teleological or the meaning of the disease as an adaptation. This last question is usually shunned by scientists, but according to von Brueke (27): "Teleology is a lady without whom no biologist can live. Yet he is ashamed to show himself with her in public."

Can we ask the question: "Where is the weakness in schizophrenia leading to disturbances in feelings, thinking and behavior?" The answer is not to a question in that form, since schizophrenia is itself a system, not produced either by a polygenetic defect or by society alone. Since it is a system, many factors are responsible at least for the preparation of the overt diseases. Perhaps a weighted scale may be developed for a continuum; the greater the biogenetic factor, the less severe the stimulus necessary for an overt syndrome, and the lesser the biogenetic factor, the stronger the stress stimulus must be. Unfortunately, the biogenetic factor has not yet been discovered in gene studies, only indirectly assumed by studies of monozygotic twins, familial incidence, biochemical alterations, and some preliminary studies of dysfunctional biological markers such as Dr. Holzman has discovered in eye tracking deficits.

We can say that there is difficulty in maintaining organizational coherence in a pleasureless life or what has been called anhedonia; excessive dependency and deficiency in competency well below the subjects' assets in work, school or social interactions; and, finally, a vulnerable sense of self-regard or self-esteem. These deficits become clear during and after a psychotic break. It is only in those patients who seem to be destined for chronic course that we may uncover unmistakable signs of psychotic behavior in childhood.

Corresponding to the above deficiencies, there are the stress stimuli that provoke a psychotic break-up in a close relationship, a loss of dependency such as leaving home for college, or a rejection by someone important to them.

The responses to these stress stimuli can no longer be considered as one of the types usually included in the classical categories of Kraepelin, Bleuler, etc. Our own categories of schizophrenia must be confirmed by lengthy follow-up studies. These include acute schizophrenic psychoses, chronic schizophrenic psychoses—some partially reversible but many irreversible—paranoid schizophrenic psychoses, schizophrenia with convulsions, schizo-affective psychoses. The shift from one type to another and the movement of schizo-affective to manic depressive disease have yet to be evaluated. At any rate, the schizophrenic may remit from his psychosis entirely or almost completely. Whether the schizophrenic thought disorder persists during this remission is still a vexing, controversial problem.

We are also by no means sure that we can predict the outcome: steady deteriorations, deterioration in shifts following each of several acute attacks, or repeated acute attacks with little general dedifferentiation. The end results cannot yet be predicated during the acute phase.

Therapy may take many forms: pharmacotherapy with phenothiazines which are antischizophrenic and may prevent future psychoses with maintenance doses; psychotherapy in various forms; or sociotherapy within groups or a favorable hospital milieu. The drug results seem most effective against the psychotic state. As for any form of therapy, we can only state that many anecdotes are available to prove the reliability of one method or another, but hard statistical results are not available. We can state that with the changing character of the disease, the antipsychotic drugs, the increase in therapeutic optimism by psychiatrists based on their decreasing fear of schizophrenic rage, and the increased ambulation of patients thereby avoiding long-term institutionalization, the outlook for improvement and even recovery is increasing.

If we view schizophrenics from the dynamic point of view and become intrigued with the content of their thinking, we will end up in a blind alley of non-understanding; interpretations will harm rather than help these patients. Using Hughlings Jackson's paradigm, one may say that the loss of control and defective organization results in negative symptoms involving relations with other systems in reality. The positive symptoms are related to the dedifferentiation or devolution permitting previously inhibited infantile pattern to reappear.

If the clinical syndrome is as an adaptive defense against the still unknown schizophrenic process, then the shutting off from reality represents an excessive defense reaction with some lacunae within the dereistic shell. The hallucinations and delusions then represent a substitute form of thinking more pleasurable than the reality that cannot be mastered.

Using a systems method is bound to abrogate such false dichotomies or polarizations as the linear cause and effect concepts and the nature *vs* nurture conflicts. The position of the physician-observer or the investigator can be clearly defined in space and time, and by weighting the factors in multiple causations, he can improve his ability to focus accurately on his therapeutic goal. The student will have to accept a degree of indeterminacy and probability amidst a larger collective order.

This means that, in the multivariant dynamics, change in a part of the total process of any disease is linked to its causes, and that these parts can only be specified by their quantitative ranges. In all of medicine, the question, as Paul Weiss states, is not what man should do, but what he should not do to repeat his mistakes; this is what Weiss calls a sanitation of traditional frames of reference.

The major mistakes in psychiatric thinking are clearly indicated in our common vocabulary, indicating the acceptance of dichotomies, states and structures. To name a few: medical *vs* social models, reductionism *vs* humanism, endogenous *vs* exogenous, process *vs* reactionary, depressions and anxieties as states, etc. These anachronistic concepts do not express dynamic processes of multiple parts and causes associated with health or illness.

As the twentieth century nears its close, many people are asking questions about the future.* In fact all sciences are looking ahead by means of conferences, symposia and a new science called "futurology" to determine how their disciplines will fare in the next century.

Psychiatrists are probably more concerned about the future because their present is, to say the least, disquieting. We are engulfed by society's antiscientism and by general feelings of frustration and futility as American political and economic conditions are changing radically for the worse.

---

* Parts of the following section are taken from my recent monograph, *Psychiatry in Broad Perspective*. New York: Behavioral Publications, 1975.

As Offer and Freedman (28) stated, research in psychiatry is not a luxury, but it cannot offer instant solutions by limiting our energies and resources for direct attacks on specific human syndromes. We need to advance not only clinical research, but so-called basic research conducted by scientists from those disciplines that form parts of the total psychiatric field system. The history of scientific advances that spin off application to the human condition in all fields of medicine indicate the need for all forms of research, no matter how detached they seem at first from practical questions.

Unfortunately the public has little patience, and its demands for crash programs, delivering immediate gains, have been expressed by bureaucrats who advocate support of only "mission-oriented" research. The community mental health concept promised primary prevention of mental illness, an objective which lies far in the future, if even there, because of the ever-present conflict between man's drives as an evolved animal and his socialized and cultural controls.

Similarly, psychiatrists have been seduced and even forced to accept every new enterprise focused on treatment, without theory, sound methods and systems of evaluation. As a result, psychiatry has been "Riding Madly in all Directions" (29). The emphasis on quantity and equality of treatment for all has prematurely sacrificed the individuality of persons in trouble and seriously weakened sound scientific investigations. The new anti-schizophrenic, anti-depressive and anti-manic drugs have been misused widely for the relief of almost any psychological complaint, just as the "miracle" antibiotics have been demanded for conditions for which they are ineffective. But these psychotropic drugs will continue to advance our knowledge of the biochemical constituents of cerebral activities as a part of the functional analysis of disorders involved in psychiatric diseases.

The future of psychiatry hinges on changes in the shifting behaviors of man in a changing society whose eventual directions we cannot predict at this time. Shifts in family constellations from the extended to the nuclear family, increased urbanization, changes in the kind of parenting, and other social and economic factors may result in changes in the kinds of coping available to succeeding generations.

Although epidemiology is important for psychiatric research, giving us estimates of incidence and prevalence of mental illnesses—including those not in therapy—and an estimation of their distribution in various social classes, we are confronted by problems of taxonomy or standardization of diagnosis. Many psychiatrists are resistant to statistics and fearful of psychiatric registries. Yet institutions must attempt to do what is now impossible, namely, to document their utility.

We cannot reorganize society; we are novices in politics, and we have not yet caught up with the explosive progress in biological psychiatry enough to develop a modern neuropsychiatry. As Arthur (30) states: "Social psychiatry, which includes the study of the impingement of social phenomena upon the genesis, manifestations, and treatment of mental and physical illness, has in recent decades become an increasingly important part of psychiatry. The epidemiology and taxonomy of mental illness, social factors in the onset and course of disease, transcultural psychiatry, the hospital viewed in social terms, and community psychiatry are all fields that have shown great expansion. But, thus far, the results of the experiences of community psychiatry and of social psychiatric studies have played a major role in the development of a crisis of identity within the profession of psychiatry, and the appropriate education and professional activities for a psychiatrist are presently in dispute."

All of this means that psychiatry is necessarily part of the process of change, at least in diagnosis, treatment and possibly in preventive measures. All the more reason why solid, well concerned research in all disciplines of psychiatry should be supported and greatly extended if our civilization is not to nurture the seeds of its own destruction. We no longer can afford the luxury of making public generalizations for narcissistic purposes.

The future rests on goals and methods of educational process to which the young aspirants are exposed. Unfortunately there are many obstacles based on outside pressures over which we have only limited control.

If we can get the student to recognize that there are no dichotomies between genetics and environment, no sharp differentiation between levels of development, and no independence of any phases of the life cycle, I think that we will have accomplished what might be called the philosophy of ontology in relation to scientific disciplines and to the therapeutic aspects of medicine (31).

This points to a new direction for a curriculum of education which, as can be seen from this outline, is multidisciplinary and primarily, but not entirely, medical. Some of it should be incorporated in the university, some in the premedical years; at least it is perceived as a continuous process. The purpose is to give to the student a concept of the totality of the life cycle, the transactional relationship among its parts, and the components of the parts—to avoid reductionism on the hand and a distorted "humanism" on the other. If we could include contributions from the scientific disciplines along with the specialties of the applied medical sciences, then, even though there are a variety of approaches and differences of methods, the total picture could give meaning to a concept of all of life, containing so-called healthy and sick components (32). This is an example of unitary thinking.

REFERENCES

1. GRINKER, R. R., SR.: A psychoanalytic historical island in Chicago (1911-1912). *Arch. Gen. Psychiatry*, 8:392-464, 1963.
2. GRINKER, R. R., SR.: Psychoanalytic theory and psychosomatic research. In J. Marmoston and E. Stainbrook (Eds.): *Psychoanalysis and the Human Situation*. New York: Vantage Press, 1964.
3. GRINKER, R. R., SR.: The Institute for Psychosomatic and Psychiatric Research and Training, Michael Reese Hospital, Chicago. *Mental Hospitals*, 7:27, 1956.
4. GRINKER, R. R., SR. and SPIEGEL, J. P.: *Men Under Stress*. Philadelphia: Blakiston, 1945.
5. GRINKER, R. R., SR.: A theoretical and experimental approach to problems of anxiety. *Arch. Neurol. Psych.*, 76:420-431, 1956.
6. GRINKER, R. R., SR.: Psychosomatic approach to anxiety. *American J. Psych.*, Vol. 113, No. 5, 1956.
7. HAMBURG, ET AL.: Classification and rating of emotional experiences. *Arch. Neurol. Psych.*, 79:415, 1958.
8. GRINKER, R. R., SR.: The physiology of emotions. In A. Simon, C. C. Herbert, and R. Straus (Eds.): *The Physiology of Emotions*. Springfield, Illinois: C C Thomas, 1961.
9. BASOWITZ, H., PERSKY, H., KORCHIN, S., and GRINKER, R. R., SR.: *Anxiety and Stress*. New York: Blakiston, 1955.
10. PERSKY, H., ET AL.: Adrenal cortical function in anxious human subjects. *Arch. Neurol. Psych.*, 76:549, 1956.
11. PERSKY, H., GRINKER, R. R., SR., and MIRSKY, I. A.: The excretion of hippuric acid in subjects with free anxiety. *J. Clin. Investigation*, 29:110, 1956.
12. GRINKER, R. R., SR.: *Psychosomatic Research*. New York: W. W. Norton, 1953. Revised edition, New York: Jason Aronson, 1973.
13. HARROWER, M. and GRINKER, R. R., SR.: The stress tolerance test utilizing both meaningful and meaningless stimuli. *Psychosomatic Medicine*, 8:3, 1946.
14. GRINKER, R. R., SR. (Ed.): *Toward a Unified Theory of Human Behavior*, second edition. New York: Basic Books, 1967.
15. GRINKER, R. R., SR.: "Open-system" psychiatry. *Amer. J. Psychoanal.*, 26:115, 1966.
16. GRINKER, R. R., SR.: "Mentally healthy" young males (homoclites). *Arch. Gen. Psych.*, 6:405, 1962.
17. GRINKER, R. R., SR. and WERBLE, B.: Mentally healthy young men (homoclites) 14 years later. *Arch. Gen. Psych.*, 30:701-709, 1974.
18. GRINKER, R. R., SR., MILLER, J., SABSHIN, M., NUNN, R., and NUNNALLY, J. C.: *The Phenomena of Depressions*. New York: Paul B. Hoeber, Inc., 1961.
19. GRINKER, R. R., SR., WERBLE, B., and DRYE, R. C.: *The Borderline Syndrome*. New York: Basic Books, 1968.

20. GRINKER, R. R., SR. and HOLZMAN, P.: Schizophrenic pathology in young adults. *Arch. Gen. Psych.*, 28:168-179, 1973.
21. GRINKER, R. R., SR.: *Clinical Introduction to S. J. Beck: The Six Schizophrenias*. New York: Grune and Stratton, 1952.
22. GRINKER, R. R., SR.: Anxiety as a significant variable for a unitary theory of human behavior. *Arch. Gen. Psych.*, 1:537-546, 1959.
23. GRINKER, R. R., SR.: Diagnosis and schizophrenia. In R. Cancro (Ed.): *The Schizophrenic Reactions*. New York: Brunner/Mazel, 1970.
24. MACFIE CAMPBELL, C.: *Destiny in Disease in Mental Disorders with Special Reference to Schizophrenia*. New York: W. W. Norton and Co., 1935.
25. SELYE, H.: The evolution of the stress concept. *American Scientist*, 61:692-698, 1973.
26. GRINKER, R. R., SR.: Changing styles in psychiatric syndromes. *Amer. J. Psych.*, 130:147-155, 1973.
27. VON BRUEKE, C. Quoted in Cannon, W.: *The Way of an Investigator: A Scientist's Experience in Medical Research*. New York: W. W. Norton and Co., 1945.
28. OFFER, D. and FREEDMAN, D. X. (Eds.): *Modern Psychiatry and Clinical Research*. New York: Basic Books, 1972.
29. GRINKER, R. R., SR.: Psychiatry rides madly in all directions. *Amer. J. Psych.*, 130:147-155, 1964.
30. ARTHUR, R. J.: *Social Psychiatry: An Overview*. Washington, D. C.: Navy Medical Neuropsychiatric Research Unit Report #73-74, 1973.
31. GRINKER, R. R., SR.: Biomedical education as a system. *Arch. Gen. Psych.*, 24:291-297, 1971.
32. GRINKER, R. R., SR.: Normality viewed as a system. *Arch. Gen. Psych.*, 17:320, 1967.

2

Genetic Considerations in the Etiology and Prevention of Schizophrenia

Robert Cancro, M.D., Med.D.Sc.

Psychiatry, more than most medical specialties, suffers from fads. In its effort to understand the origins of human behavior, it has vacillated amongst a number of simplistic alternatives. The desire to achieve scientific immortality has driven some theorists to extreme and exclusive positions. The so-called purely organic and purely psychogenic schools have been most guilty of ascientific, if not antiscientific, polemics. The mutual exclusiveness of these positions seems to reflect the biases and narcissistic needs of the theorists more than the demands of knowledge. There is no true conflict between biology and psychology, although it is easy for men to create a false one. The need is to synthesize these exclusive positions into a comprehensive and testable theory.

It may be helpful to review briefly the history of the clinical concept of dementia praecox and some of its vicissitudes (1). The term was introduced in 1852 by Morel (2) to describe a single case of dementia in which the onset occurred during adolescence. He did not presume this label described a disease entity, but rather that it identified remarkable features of the condition of his young patient. Despite Morel's caution, the psychiatry of that period was under the influence of men like Griesinger (3) and dominated by etiologic concepts such as brain disease, moral degeneracy, and constitutional weakness. In 1899 Kraepelin (4) used the term as one of the two major divisions of the endogenous psychoses. The basis of the division was the presence or absence of deterioration. Despite his later concession that all patients with dementia praecox need not go on to deteriorate, the division stood firm in clinical practice. Kraepelin's conceptualization of dementia praecox included the cases described almost a century earlier by Pinel (5) and Haslam (6). He also included the cases identified by Hecker (7) and Kahlbaum (8) as hebephrenia and catatonia, respectively. These terms were no longer adjectives but had become nouns, i.e., the names of discrete and real entities.

Bleuler's (9) major work on dementia praecox appeared in 1911, only twelve years after Kraepelin's classic division. Bleuler argued that the term was misleading, since the onset of the illness did not have to occur during puberty and the course did not lead inevitably to deterioration. He did more than change the name. He moved towards a syndrome concept by suggesting that dementia praecox consisted of a group of disorders with similar symptomatology. This was an important step away from the disease entity model of Kraepelin.

Meyer (10) took a more interactional view of this disorder, seeing it as a reaction to the environment. His stress on the life chart of the patient explicitly contained the concept of a person reacting to environmental situations with psychologic symptoms. This approach to mental illness remained strong in the United States until the 1968 revision of *The Diagnostic and Statistical Manual* (11). It defines schizophrenia in the following fashion:

This large category includes a group of disorders manifested by characteristic disturbances of thinking, mood and behavior. Disturbances in thinking are marked by alterations of concept formation which may lead to misinterpretation of reality and sometimes to delusions and hallucinations, which frequently appear psychologically self-protective. Corollary mood changes include ambivalent, constricted and inappropriate emotional responsiveness and loss of empathy with others. Behavior may be withdrawn, regressive and bizarre.

As we review the history of the concept we are struck by the marked fluctuations. It has been considered everything from a single disease to a way of life that transcends the conventional narrow boundaries of reality. The prognosis has been described as everything from universally poor to better than most neuroses. Every effort to improve the nosological confusion has subsequently led further into the morass. It is no surprise that the student is puzzled. In 1968 American psychiatry agreed to an internationally accepted classification. It specifies that schizophrenia is a group of disorders, i.e., illnesses. Not only is schizophrenia defined as an illness, but the signs and symptoms by which it can be diagnosed are listed. The student can learn to identify the particular signs and symptoms, and then label the individuals who show them as schizophrenic. While it is easy to understand the desire for nosological clarity, it is doubtful that we have gained much with this new/old emphasis. It is a frighteningly static and cross-sectional view of illness as an entity which ignores both its adaptive function and its process. The static clinical picture described in *The Diagnostic and Statistical Manual* is the end state of an adaptive process which has not been wholly successful. As we know from the principle of equifinality, this end state can be arrived at from a number of different initial conditions and through a variety of pathways. The important diagnostic versus classificatory goal is increasing the reliability of the identification of a particular group of end states as schizophrenia. Yet it is vital to understand that this increased reliability does not improve either the validity of the diagnostic category or the usefulness of the classification in comprehending the process. Is schizophrenia an end state whose clinical picture we can describe? Is it the process of reaching that end state? Or both?

It is helpful to remember the distinction between diagnosis and classification (12). A diagnosis is a statement of what is troubling a person at a given time, in a specified fashion, and in a particular context. It is an effort to merge general knowledge about illness with specific knowledge about the individual as a means of helping that person. A classification is quite different. It is an attempt to organize the data into a comprehensible system which matches the mode of our cognitive functioning. The ordering of data, for example, in classes and subclasses is not a function of nature but of our cognitive apparatus. It is the way we think and, therefore, the way we organize data. Classification is an essential method of science as performed by man and intends to impose our understanding on the data by ordering it in this particular fashion. An increase in reliability is a legitimate diagnostic goal, since diagnosis emphasizes the end state. This task, if accomplished, would, however, yield little of value to classification, since classification emphasizes the process. This distinction between diagnosis and classification helps us to phrase the two questions mentioned earlier more clearly. Does the concept of schizophrenia as it is officially defined have validity as a diagnostic category? Does it help to improve our understanding of the process of this disorder?

In addressing the first question it is necessary to realize that the anguish found in most patients labeled schizophrenic is not mythology but madness. Yet, we can wonder about the homogeneity if not the existence of the grouping. Certainly there are enormous clinical variations amongst people so labeled. It is helpful to understand that the current official definition of schizophrenia is not useful if one conceives of the disorder as a single disease. The variation is too great for this category to include only one type of illness (13). When we think of the category as a group or class of related end states that have been arrived at through different pathways from different initial conditions, we see that the category has some limited diagnostic usefulness. This utility should not be confused with independent validation. We do not have an equivalent to the glucose tolerance test for schizophrenia. Until we do, diagnosis and classification will remain separate.

While the category is of some value for diagnostic purposes, it is of virtually no aid in increasing our understanding of the process (14). We cannot infer the pathway nor the initial condition from the end state. We can draw some conclusions, however, concerning the patient's need to find a new dynamic steady state to his environment at the time of his psychotic decompensation. His previous adaptation could no longer serve. The precise nature of the changes which exceeded the reserves of the earlier nonpsychotic adaptation is not known. The changes could have been any combination of chemical, intrapsychic, interpersonal, or social variables. We do know that there was a need for a new organism-environment dynamic steady state, and the process of achieving the new steady state can be called schizophrenia. Clearly, the more desirable goal is to understand the process better and not just to describe the end state more lucidly. Yet there is value in knowing that a particular end state was achieved as opposed to some other. For this reason alone, improving diagnostic reliability is useful.

The well-known problems of diagnostic reliability are in part a function of differences in recognizing and labeling a particular end state as schizophrenic (15-19). For the remainder of the paper the term schizophrenia will be used only in the sense of an end state. There has, of course, been a considerable lack of agreement on those criteria which are essential. Many clinicians still make the diagnosis on the basis of an intuitive feeling they have about the patient. This cannot be an adequate basis for increasing the homogeneity of the population labeled schizophrenic. Since 1911 the fundamental signs in schizophrenia have been considered to be autism, ambivalence, the affective disturbance, and the associational disturbance. However, autism, ambivalence, and many of the affective disturbances seen in schizophrenia are not exclusive to the disorder. Any of these can be found to a greater or lesser degree in a variety of individuals including so-called normals. It is the particular cognitive disturbance that is probably unique to schizophrenia. For this reason it would appear wise to restrict the category to patients who show a characteristic thought disorder (20). In this sense *The Diagnostic and Statistical Manual* makes a real contribution since it does restrict the diagnosis to the thought-disordered patients.

The evidence for the existence of a genetic contribution to the etiology of schizophrenia, particularly its prevalence, is so strong as no longer to be in reasonable doubt. This does not mean that there are not individuals who deny it. It simply means there is no reasonable basis, in my judgment, for their conclusion.

There are three main lines of evidence for a genetic factor which will be summarized: the consanguinity, twin, and adoptive studies. The consanguinity studies consistently show that the prevalence of schizophrenia is significantly higher in the genetic relatives of schizophrenic patients than it is in the general population. This has been found in every such study published, including those done by investigators with a markedly environmental bias (21). (The relative stability of the prevalence rate in the general population both within and between many cultures argues, in itself, for a genetic factor.) More important than the simple finding is the significant positive relationship between the frequency of the disorder and the degree of kinship. The closer the genetic relationship to the patient, the more likely it is that the relative will show the disorder. For the parents, siblings, and children of schizophrenics, the prevalence is approximately 10-15 percent, while it is less than 1 percent in the general population. Even second-order relatives show a significantly higher risk than the general population, although not as high as closer relatives.

Clearly, the consanguinity studies are a weak form of evidence. They can just as validly be interpreted as supporting an environmental explanation. The environmentalist can argue that the closer the degree of kinship, the more intense the psychologic relationship between the individuals and, therefore, the more likely that they shared similar predisposing environmental experiences. Yet there is a little-known study which offers evidence for a genetic factor in the course, and not just the prevalence, of the disorder. Bleuler (22) reported that the relatives who also had schizophrenia tended to have the same type of onset, symptomatology, duration of illness, and outcome. While this finding can be interpreted in either an environmental or genetic fashion, the more parsimonious explanation is genetic, since many of the relatives were geographically well separated, and in some cases did not even know each other.

The twin studies have been helpful in adding a stronger body of evidence. The concordance rate for schizophrenia in monozygotic twins has consistently been found to be significantly higher than the rate in dizygotic twins. The earlier studies found concordance rates in monozygotic twins of 60-86 percent (21). Unfortunately they had certain methodologic failings, not the least of which was that the index case was found in a chronic hospital population representing the worst prognostic group. More recent studies have been extended to larger populations of dizygotic twins, thereby including index cases who were less severely ill (23-26). The concordance rate in these efforts varies between 6-40 percent. The exact percentage is primarily a function of the diagnostic criteria used. The more recent investigations include the total population of twins and are, therefore, methodologically superior. The concordance rate in all the studies of dizygotic twins has been no higher than for siblings. Rosenthal (27) reviewed eleven twin studies and found that in ten the concordance rates were consistent with the predictions that would be made from genetic theory. Interestingly, in the study done by Pollin (28) on 16,000 twin pairs collected by the National Academy of Sciences from the Veterans Administration, there was a systematic bias in the direction of health. Pollin's sample included only those twins who had passed the induction screening and served in the armed forces. If one or both members of the twin pair were rejected for military service, they were not included in the sample. This procedure resulted in a population in which the psychotic decompensations of late adolescence and early adulthood were excluded. This naturally produced a lower concordance rate for the monozygotic twins. Nevertheless, the concordance rate in the monozygotic twins in this sample was three times higher than in the dizygotic twins. Pollin's study also showed no significant difference in concordance between monozygotic and dizygotic pairs for psychoneuroses.

A pure psychologic theory can still explain the twin data without having to be stretched too far. Monozygotic twins share more than their genetic makeup. There is a very special relationship between them which contributes to the formation of a strong mutual identification. They are frequently mistaken for each other, dressed alike, called by each other's name, etc. All of these experiences can contribute to a very special environment in which what one does is likely to be repeated by the other. The occurrence of identical twins who have been reared separately helps to clarify the problem. There are sixteen reported cases of monozygotic twins reared apart in which one of the twins was diagnosed as schizophrenic (21). The concordance rate for this group was 62.5 percent and is comparable, for a sample of this small size, to that found in monozygotic twins reared together. This finding is very supportive for the existence of a genetic factor.

The most important and compelling line of evidence comes from studies in which the parent and child generations have been separated so that the child is not reared by the biologic parent. The first such study published was by Heston (29). In a well-controlled investigation, he examined the prevalence of schizophrenia in the offspring of schizophrenic women. These children had been adopted early in life by nonschizophrenic parents. As a control group he used the children of nonschizophrenic women who had also been adopted. It was the offspring of schizophrenic women who showed the significantly higher rate of schizophrenia and, more interestingly, showed a rate which did not differ significantly from that which would have been expected if they had been raised by their biologic mothers. Kety, Rosenthal, Wender, and Schulsinger (30) approached the problem from a related but somewhat different direction. They took a large population of adopted children and separated them into those who became or did not become schizophrenic. They then ascertained the prevalence of schizophrenia in the biologic versus the adoptive relatives of the schizophrenic children. They studied all children adopted in Copenhagen in a 24-year period. They also excluded all adoptions by individuals who were biologically related to the true parents. They, too, found a significantly higher prevalence of schizophrenia and schizophrenia-like disorders in the biologic relatives. One very important finding in their study was that approximately half of the biologic relatives of index cases who showed schizophrenia spectrum disorders were paternal half-siblings and, therefore, did not share with the index case a common uterus. This finding was evidence for a relatively pure genetic factor which was independent of the expected range of variation in the early intrauterine environment. It must be remembered that in the behavioral sciences we are dealing with evidence and not proof. Our hypotheses cannot be proven in a rigorous mathematical sense, but the weight of the evidence can be sufficiently strong that we can, for practical purposes, consider them proven. When one reflects on the evidence from the consanguinity, twin, and adoptive studies, it is obvious that a genetic factor in the prevalence of schizophrenia has been demonstrated beyond reasonable doubt. Unfortunately, existence and understanding are not coextensive and we are still faced by the more difficult question of what the genetic studies mean.

In all the furor that has gone on in recent years concerning the existence and/or relative importance of a genetic factor in the etiology of schizophrenia, there has been a remarkable lack of discussion concerning the quality of the evidence for the existence of an environmental factor. This evidence will be very briefly reviewed. It has long been known that there is a relationship between social class and the prevalence of schizophrenia (31). The disorder is found more frequently amongst the poor. While this can be interpreted as evidence for the role of impoverished social conditions in the etiology of schizophrenia, it can be explained equally well by the schizophrenics' tendency to drift down the socioeconomic ladder because of their inability to compete effectively.

The marked increase in interest in the study of families has resulted in careful examination of how children are affected by parental psychopathology and disordered communication patterns within families. The claim has been that schizophrenic children are the product of seriously and characteristically disturbed families. These studies have suffered from several methodologic limitations including the relative absence of normal control families. Usually the observers were aware of the diagnosis of the index case, and this knowledge could have easily caused them to overemphasize family interactions which might otherwise have been considered insignificant. Another methodologic problem was that the families were observed after the child had become psychotic, so that it was not certain that the disordered patterns preceded rather than followed the schizophrenic illness. A clever device for avoiding certain of the problems of halo effect was to score projective tests blindly. Wynne (32) and co-workers have demonstrated significant group differences between the Rorschachs of the parents of schizophrenic and normal children. There are, however, still methodologic problems with this approach, since the psychological tester was not blind to the diagnosis. This knowledge in turn could have influenced the projective test data which were gathered (33).

The important issue is that most of the environmental data can support a genetic theory equally well. This is precisely the situation with much of the genetic data. It is relatively nonspecific. Kety (34) argued that: "The most incontrovertible evidence that non-genetic factors operate in the etiology of schizophrenia is the fact that the concordance rate for schizophrenia in monozygotic twins is considerably less than 100 percent." He went on to add that the concordance rate of 40-50 percent in the newer genetic studies leaves "a large area for the operation of factors other than genetic . . . ." The moderate concordance rate tells us very little about the size of either the environmental or genetic factor. The monozygotic concordance rate is not an expression of the strength of the genetic influence. It is the significance of the difference between the monozygotic and dizygotic rates which determines the existence of a genetic factor. It is very difficult to divide genetic and environmental factors into separate parcels, however. The biologic reality is that it is essential to have both a genotype and an evoking environment. Since both are necessary, it is difficult to speak of relative importance except in the very limited and specific sense expressed by a heritability index. The best theoretical argument for the existence of environmental factors is that they are necessary for the genes to be activated. The traditional distinction between genetic factor and determination is essential. Having a particular genetic makeup does not determine the outcome inevitably. It takes more than a particular genotype to produce schizophrenia. The concordance rate confirms this fact clearly and is also reassuring in the sense that, without any planned manipulation, a monozygotic twin has less than a 40 percent chance of developing the disorder when his co-twin has been so diagnosed. When we realize that there must be a number of monozygotic twin pairs who have the genotype necessary for vulnerability but of whom neither develops the disorder, we can see the risk is probably even less.

As indicated earlier, there is no better argument for the presence of an environmental factor than our knowledge that it must exist for the specific genotype to be activated. The environment determines which of the many genes will be enhanced and which will be suppressed. In this special sense the environment determines the effective or operational genotype. Part of the confusion results from the word "environment" being used in multiple senses. It means everything from the concentration of critical nutrients in the maternal bloodstream to familial rearing patterns. It would be best if we expressed the role of environmental variables in terms that allowed us to understand their interaction with the genotype more adequately. For the time being, this remains more of an aspiration than a reality in schizophrenia. A great deal of research must still be done which specifies the particular environmental—including social and psychologic—variables, the timing of their interaction, and the precise physiologic pathways through which they selectively activate the genome to produce one of the possible phenotypic outcomes. There have been promising environmental leads ranging from family interaction patterns to nutrition. There is considerable evidence in the case of intelligence to suggest that prenatal nutrition, early infant handling, and patterns of sensory stimulation play a role in its development. The family studies done with schizophrenic patients suggest that, at least in some cases, aberrant patterns of social interaction play a role in the development of the disorder. There is evidence concerning the possible role of cereal substances in the exacerbation of schizophrenic symptoms which should not be dismissed out of hand (35). While it is true that every other such finding has been subsequently demonstrated to be an artifact, it is inevitable that some will eventually prove to be valid.

The environment is critical in the etiology of schizophrenia for exactly the same reason that the genetic component is, i.e., they are both necessary. The question of relative importance, as mentioned earlier, may at present be more academic than practical. It has often been said that the genotype is necessary but not sufficient. While the statement is literally true, it is better to conceive of the genotype as one member of an interacting series of causal events which produces the vulnerability to the disorder. We may by choice divide the members of the series into two categories called genetic and environmental. This division is helpful pedagogically. It is an error to reify this division and then treat the categories as separate sources of independent variance. The interaction between gene and environment necessary to produce any phenotype is a reality of biology, and this reality is not captured in the mathematical model of an analysis of variance. Mathematical models of gene-environment interaction are possible, but good ones are not presently available.

The concept of norm of reaction and the highly related one of phenoptions address themselves to the degrees of freedom existing in the genotype. The genotype can produce a relatively broad range of phenotypes as a function of differences in the environment, although there are inherent limitations as well. In practice the variation in environments to which a genotype is exposed tends to be small. It is helpful to utilize the concept of the most probable environment to which the genotype will be exposed (36). Given the most probable environment, we can predict with relative certainty the phenotype that will be produced. If the genotype is exposed to highly improbable environments, it becomes increasingly likely that the phenotype will differ from that produced by the most probable environment. Much research is needed to identify the environments which will prevent the several genotypes from unfolding in the direction of vulnerability to a schizophrenic illness. Even if this research were to be successful it still might be of limited therapeutic value, since there is no a priori reason to assume that the environments which prevent are those which suppress schizophrenia. When we take these facts into account, we need not be apologetic for the contribution of the environment. It is more a function of scientists than of science that we argue about the relative contributions of our respective disciplines to important problems. The geneticist and the clinician both have something of value to offer. It is not essential except as an exercise in narcissism for either to be more important.

There are several possible modes of inheritance which fit the observed data. My personal preference is for a polygenic model involving a small number of genes, in the range of two to four. There is also good reason to assume that there is more than a single genetic constellation which can produce this clinical disorder. In other words, there is a moderate but finite number of gene combinations, each utilizing several—not necessarily the same—genes which are isophenic.

If we utilize a polygenic model of the mode of inheritance, we should not expect an abnormal phenotype but rather are forced in a different direction. It is critical to understand that in this model schizophrenia is *not* a phenotype but an end state that involves the presence of two or more phenotypic characteristics. This conceptualization proposes that there are no abnormal phenotypes in schizophrenia but rather a statistically unusual pattern or array of phenotypes. If we assume that the traits in question are distributed on a normal curve, then one third of the population will be beyond one standard deviation from the mean for each trait. (Parenthetically, the number of individuals in one specific direction from the mean of the distribution for two traits would equal 2.78% of the general population or approximately three times the prevalence rate of schizophrenia.) The ends of the distribution of any trait represent the more uncommon but nevertheless normal variants. A predictable percentage of a population will have a statistically unusual cluster of extreme scores on these traits. We are assuming that there are one or more such patterns which predispose or represent the vulnerability to schizophrenia. An example of a phenotype likely to be implicated, in my judgment, comes out of the cognitive control tradition and is the individual's characteristic distribution of attention between internal and external sources of stimuli. These same individuals in a different environment would have either the same or a different pattern evoked, leaving them vulnerable to schizophrenia or some other genetically related disorder, respectively. Heston's (29) work suggests that alcoholism and psychopathy may be phenoptions or phenotypic alternatives to schizophrenia. The majority of the vulnerable individuals never decompensate and may even have certain adaptive advantages over those individuals whose patterns are more common.

A few general remarks on treatment are in order. More than a score of years have passed since the introduction of chlorpromazine, and the clinical use of antipsychotic drugs remains irrational. The single greatest abuse in my experience is polypharmacy. Our patients should not be given every drug just

GENETIC CONSIDERATIONS

because it's there. Pharmacotherapy does not replace social rehabilitation, which is essential in most schizophrenics. The task of rehabilitation requires the development of human relationships which involve trust and closeness. If we dread getting close to the schizophrenic and prefer to keep him at a proper obtunded distance, we should not impose our anxiety on him and call it treatment. Drugs cannot replace contact and involvement.

The feasibility and legitimacy of preventing schizophrenia are complex questions involving both technical and moral issues. The social and individual benefits are obvious, the costs less so. Both the costs and benefits must be clearly identified and weighed prior to our taking any steps, no matter how well-intentioned. There are two promising methods for reducing the occurrence of schizophrenia in the population through genetic manipulation. The first of these is genetic engineering. Presently this is a topic which is more suitable for the Sunday Supplement than for science. While the ability to alter the molecular structure of genes is not imminent, it is highly probable that it will become so in the future. Unfortunately, there is little doubt that, when it does arrive, we shall do as we have always done in the past, which is to use promptly any scientific development that comes along. A presently available alternative is genetic counseling or its more extreme version, eugenics, which can alter the gene pool through discouragement of reproduction in schizophrenics and, thereby, reduce the frequency of schizophrenia in the population. The increasing reproductive rate in schizophrenics brought about by shortened hospital stays and the effort to encourage patients to lead more normal social lives will result in a higher prevalence rate of schizophrenia in future generations (37). This is a predictable negative consequence of our current therapeutic activities in this disorder. Nothing is being done to counter this effect on the future generations. Genetic counseling is not routinely practiced with schizophrenic patients. Even if it were, it is far from clear how effective it would be with, for example, a chronically psychotic individual. Genetic counseling may be sufficient with potential parents who are able to comprehend the issues involved and do not wish to take unnecessary risks. There is much reason to believe that the cognitive disturbance and impaired reality testing in schizophrenics would render genetic counseling ineffective.

If we wish to lower the prevalence rate of schizophrenia through genetic manipulation, we have to face the very real likelihood that counseling will not be enough. On an individual basis, does the risk of an occurrence which is less than 15 percent justify the denial of parenthood? On a broader basis, does society have the right to control parenthood? These are the critical moral questions for whose answering physicians are no better prepared than nonphysicians. We can, however, contribute some knowledge which, while not directly answering the moral questions, may be helpful in addressing them.

The major risk in manipulating the gene pool is the danger of its permanent alteration. If a gene is bred out of a population, it may be impossible to reintroduce it. The negative consequences of breeding out an undesirable gene or even reducing its frequency may not be apparent until it is too late. Obviously, the problem is grossly magnified if the genes are normal. There are a number of studies, for example, which suggest that creativity and schizophrenia are linked. If so-called eugenic practices were to reduce the prevalence of schizophrenia at the cost of reducing the level of creativity in the population, we would indeed be facing a dilemma. It is difficult if not impossible to predict accurately the cost of any given genetic manipulation. The inescapable conclusion is that it is dangerous to meddle with the gene pool. This simple rule of "nonaction" extends beyond the small group labeled schizophrenic. Yet we must face the equally real fact that, in the name of our humane concern for people, we have in the last thirty years influenced the human gene pool in very profound ways through social legislation and medical advances. Social legislation has made it possible for a number of people, including schizophrenics, to reproduce and for their offspring to survive, who otherwise would not have done so. This enlightened social legislation has been primarily restricted to the technologically advanced countries, but the benefits of modern medicine have spread even to the underdeveloped nations. The introduction of antibiotics and the other medical advances since World War II have kept large numbers of individuals alive who in the past would not have survived long enough to contribute offspring. In a very real sense the development of penicillin and DDT, with the resulting control of many lethal diseases, has had more impact on the gene pool than any other development in the recent history of the species. The rapidly increasing world population is clear evidence of this impact. It is not enough to argue that our previous and present manipulations are in a different class since they have been to save lives. Obviously, good intentions are not an adequate justification. We are altering the genetic makeup of Homo sapiens as a population and doing it without plan. Perhaps this "nonplan" is to be preferred, but at the least we should recognize what is being done and consider the alternatives.

The issues raised go far beyond the limited question of schizophrenia. Yet the need for rationally determined analyses of costs and benefits is the same. It is here that science can contribute without violating the democratic process. The decisions rest with the body politic, and science must not only identify the costs and benefits but must communicate them effectively and fairly to the populace.

One way of influencing the phenotype without the dangers inherent in altering the gene pool is through environmental manipulation. A disadvantage is that the environmental manipulation would have to be repeated with every generation. Most observers find this approach more emotionally palatable, since it can be rationalized as equalizing rather than manipulating the environment. This position represents more of a semantic deception than a humanistic advance. Before developing this point further, it is well we reemphasize another limitation in this approach, since the environment that may evoke vulnerability to schizophrenia in certain individuals may evoke socially valuable traits in others with similar genetic endowments. The critical deficiency in our desire to equalize the environment in the sense of making it the same is that it does not result in the identical phenotype. Individual differences in the phenotype will still occur, but they will be solely on the basis of genetic differences. If we want to equalize the environment in the sense of influencing the phenotype, we shall have to identify environments that are equally evocative or equally suppressive in *different* individuals. We cannot even assume that the environment that suppresses a schizophrenic predisposition in one person is necessarily going to suppress it in another. Schizophrenia is not a homogeneous entity but rather an end state (or a group of clinically similar end states) in which the vulnerability can be arrived at either from a number of different genotypes or else through a variety of different gene interactions. We may be fortunate and find that there are a relatively small, or at the very least a finite, number of environmental manipulations which would prevent the disorder. While we believe certain environments to be noxious, the data from the adopted-child studies show that being raised in a nonschizophrenic home does not significantly lower the prevalence of the disorder in the offspring of schizophrenic parents. This does not mean that the environment is unimportant. The most parsimonious explanation is that the genetic-environment interactions which produce the vulnerability are prenatal, and the developmental stresses and tasks which produce the decompensation are statistically as likely in a nonschizophrenic as in a schizophrenic home. This suggests that the environmental tasks which evoke the illness are quite ubiquitous and likely to be encountered by most individuals in the culture. The equalization of the environment then might involve considerable alteration if we are to succeed in our effort to prevent the disorder. We must create highly improbable environments to reduce further the prevalence rate of schizophrenia. Even if we were to identify such environments, we would have to deal with the question of the cost involved in imposing them. For example, if a child had to be taken from his natural or adoptive parents and raised by trained caretakers in special settings for high-risk children, he would have paid a high price for his vaccination. The actual damage done to the children by the techniques of prevention must be weighed against the potential benefits. This is a particularly difficult choice when we realize that the beneficiaries of the prevention number at most merely 15 percent of the population so treated. In our eagerness to prevent the schizophrenic psychosis we must not do more harm to a group of people whom we have unintentionally injured repeatedly. In the foreseeable future, adequate treatment and rehabilitation offer more benefits at lower costs than any form of primary prevention.

REFERENCES

1. CANCRO, R. and PRUYSER, P. W.: A historical review of the development of the concept of schizophrenia. *Bull. Menn. Clinic*, 34:61-70, 1970.
2. MOREL, B. A.: *Études Cliniques: Traité Théorique et Pratique des Maladies Mentales*. Paris: Masson, 1852-1853.
3. GRIESINGER, W.: *Die Pathologie und Therapie der Psychischen Krankheiten*. Braunschweig, Wreden, 1871.
4. KRAEPELIN, E.: *Psychiatrie. Ein Lehrbuch für Studierende und Ärzte*, 6th ed. Leipzig, Barth, 1899.
5. PINEL, P.: *Traité Medico-Philosophique sur l'Aliénation Mentale, ou la Manie*. Paris: Richard, Caille et Ravier, 1801.
6. HASLAM, J.: *Observations on Madness and Melancholy*, 2nd ed. London: Hayden, 1809.

7. HECKER, E.: Die Hebephrenie. *Arch für pathol Anat u Physiol u klinische Med*, 52:394, 1871.
8. KAHLBAUM, K. L.: *Die Katatonie oder das Spannungsirresein.* Berlin: Hirschwald, 1874.
9. BLEULER, E.: *Dementia Praecox or the Group of the Schizophrenias.* New York: Int. Univ. Press, 1950.
10. MEYER, A.: The life chart and the obligation of specifying positive data in psychopathological diagnosis. In E. E. Winters (Ed.): *The Collected Papers of Adolf Meyer.* Baltimore: Johns Hopkins, 1951, vol. III.
11. American Psychiatric Association: *Diagnostic and Statistical Manual of Mental Disorders*, 2nd ed. Washington, 1968.
12. MENNINGER, K., MAYMAN, M., and PRUYSER, P. W.: *The Vital Balance.* New York: Viking, 1963.
13. CANCRO, R.: A review of current research directions: Their product and their promise. In R. Cancro (Ed.): *The Schizophrenic Reactions: A Critique of the Concept, Hospital Treatment, and Current Research.* New York: Brunner/Mazel, 1970.
14. CANCRO, R.: Increased diagnostic reliability in schizophrenia: Some values and limitations. *Int. J. Psychiat.*, 11:53-57, 1973.
15. HOCH, P.: The etiology and epidemiology of schizophrenia. *Amer. J. Public Health*, 47:1071, 1957.
16. KREITMAN, N.: The reliability of psychiatric diagnosis. *J. Ment. Sci.*, 107:876, 1961.
17. MEHLMAN, B.: The reliability of psychiatric diagnosis. *J. Abn. Soc. Psychol.*, 47:577, 1952.
18. PASAMANICK, B., DINITZ, S., and LEFTON, M.: Psychiatric orientation and its relation to diagnosis and treatment in a mental hospital. *Amer. J. Psychiat.*, 116:127, 1959.
19. SCHORER, C. E.: Mistakes in the diagnosis of schizophrenia. *Amer. J. Psychiat.*, 124:1057, 1968.
20. CANCRO, R.: Thought disorder and schizophrenia. *Dis. Nerv. Syst.*, 29:846, 1968.
21. SLATER, E.: A review of earlier evidence on genetic factors. In D. Rosenthal and S. S. Kety (Eds.): *The Transmission of Schizophrenia.* Oxford: Pergamon Press, 1968.
22. BLEULER, M.: *Krankheitsverlauf, Persönlichkeit und Verwandtschaft Schizophrener und ihre gegenseitige Beziehungen.* Leipzig: Thieme, 1941.
23. FISCHER, M., HARVALD, B., and HAUGE, M.: A Danish twin study of schizophrenia. *Brit. J. Psychiat.*, 115:981, 1969.
24. GOTTESMAN, I. I. and SHIELDS, J.: Schizophrenia in twins: 16 years' consecutive admissions to a psychiatric clinic. *Brit. J. Psychiat.*, 112:809, 1966.
25. KRINGLEN, E.: Schizophrenia in twins. An epidemiological-clinical study. *Psychiatry*, 29:172, 1966.
26. TIENARI, P.: Psychiatric illnesses in identical twins. *Acta Psychiat. Scand.* (Suppl), 171:1, 1963.

27. ROSENTHAL, D.: Genetic research in the schizophrenic syndrome. In Cancro, R. (Ed.): *The Schizophrenic Reactions: A Critique of the Concept, Hospital Treatment, and Current Research.* New York: Brunner/Mazel, 1970.
28. POLLIN, W., ALLEN, M., HOFFER, A., STABENAU, J., and HRUBEC, Z.: Psychopathology in 15,909 pairs of veteran twins: Evidence for a genetic factor in the pathogenesis of schizophrenia and its relative absence in psychoneuroses. *Amer. J. Psychiat.*, 126: 597, 1969.
29. HESTON, L. L.: Psychiatric disorders in foster home reared children of schizophrenic mothers. *Brit. J. Psychiat.*, 112:819, 1966.
30. KETY, S. S., ROSENTHAL, D., WENDER, P., and SCHULSINGER, F.: The types and prevalence of mental illness in the biological and adoptive families of adopted schizophrenics. In D. Rosenthal and S. S. Kety (Eds.): *The Transmission of Schizophrenia.* Oxford: Pergamon Press, 1968.
31. FARIS, R. E. L. and DUNHAM, H. W.: *Mental Disorders in Urban Areas: An Ecological Study of Schizophrenia and Other Psychoses.* Chicago: University of Chicago, 1939.
32. WYNNE, L. C.: Methodologic and conceptual issues in the study of schizophrenics and their families. In D. Rosenthal and S. S. Kety (Eds.): *The Transmission of Schizophrenia.* Oxford: Pergamon Press, 1968.
33. HIRSCH, S. R.: Abnormal language and communication in the aetiology of schizophrenia, a double-blind quantitative study. *Abstracts, Fifth World Congress of Psychiatry.* Mexico: La Prensa Médica Mexicana, 1971, p. 135.
34. KETY, S. S.: Genetic-environmental interactions in schizophrenia. *Trans. & Stud. Coll. Physicians Phil.*, 38:124, 1970.
35. DOHAN, F. C., GRASBERGER, J. C., LOWELL, F. M., JOHNSTON, H., JR., and ARBEGAST, A. W.: Relapsed schizophrenics: More rapid improvement on a milk and cereal free diet. *Brit. J. Psychiat.*, 115:595, 1969.
36. CANCRO, R.: Genetic contributions to individual differences in intelligence: An introduction. In R. Cancro (Ed.): *Intelligence: Genetic and Environmental Influences.* New York: Grune & Stratton, 1971.
37. ERLENMEYER-KIMLING, L., RAINER, J. D., and KALLMANN, F. J.: Current reproductive trends in schizophrenia. In P. H. Hoch and J. Zubin (Eds.): *Psychopathology of Schizophrenia.* New York: Grune & Stratton, 1966.

3

The Bucket, the Train, and the Feedback Loop in Biochemical Psychiatry

Arnold J. Mandell, M.D.

Research into the biochemistry of human affect has advanced dramatically since the shift of emphasis from peripheral metabolites to central synaptic mechanisms, and increased attention to the central action of drugs has begun to allow access to neurochemical correlates of clinical states. In fact, since evaluation of human behavior remains somewhat impressionistic we can specify drug-induced neurochemical changes better than we can describe subjective alterations in mood, particularly those that fall short of the extremes. One problem is that researchers are often at the mercy of their own biases: one's *dysphoria* is another's *depression;* one's *mania* is another's *aggression*. Schachter and Singer's (1962) studies of the influence of set upon the subjective experience illustrate the dilemma faced by experimental subjects. Moreover, indices like the Clyde Mood Scale, the Hamilton Scale, and the Minnesota Multiphasic Personality Inventory are only as reliable as agreements about what they measure. In view of the vastness of our ignorance, perhaps only in retrospect can we appreciate how far we have come toward an understanding of human affect through biochemistry.

Initial attempts to relate biochemical measures to such states as anxiety, fear, aggression, and depression were based on the supposition that peripheral metabolites were related directly to the metabolism of the CNS. Many investigators have tried to correlate urinary and blood hormone metabolites with indices or observed affectual states in humans and other primates. Using techniques ranging from measures in the urine to immunoassays of plasma hormones, they have related pituitary, adrenal, gonadal, and thyroid indices of function to various experimental and natural states. Variables dependent upon hormones have also been correlated with electrophysiological as well as biochemical measures of sleep.

Two kinds of information have been forthcoming from neuroendocrinological research. The first kind suggests that abnormalities in the brain (reflected by states of rage, depression, or panic) *can* be related systematically to neuroendocrinological measures; the second establishes constraints on the first by recognizing that environmental circumstances are not the sole determinants of behavioral states or changes. Individual coping strength or personal defense style and the characteristics of particular environmental impingements weigh in the balance. In the future we may develop physiochemical gauges for predicting stress tolerance, consistency of performance, and proneness to psychosomatic disease in men and women, and it may be that coming immunological techniques for studying pituitary hormones will be sophisticated enough to relate hormones to human emotional states. For example, Prange et al. (1974) and Kastin et al. (1972) have focused on an apparent association between thyroid stimulating hormone (TSH) and depression in man: they find evidence for hypothalamic dysfunction in endogenously depressed people, suggested by disturbances in pulsatile release patterns and by low levels of circulating TSH.

Beginning with the work of Elmadjian (1962), urinary and blood metabolites of the catecholamines and later of serotonin have been shown to have associations with anger and anxiety. The turnover of infused isotopic catecholamines was early related to psychopathology. Using the data of Armstrong et al. (1956) on urinary phenol metabolites of the catecholamines, Axelrod (1959) and his group first gave a metabolic accounting for the peripheral metabolism of these amines, and Kopin and Gordon (1962, 1963), Maas and Landis (1966, 1968), and Schildkraut et al. (1965) have directed studies of the kinetics of catecholamine turnover in respect to affective disorder and drug action. Psychosomatic manifestations provoked by experimental manipulations have been linked to levels of urinary catecholamines and their metabolites as well. It is becoming clear, however, that urinary and blood metabolites of putative neurotransmitters come from peripheral chromaffin tissues like that found in the adrenal medulla, the sympathetic nervous system, and the gut. These systems are far removed from the brain, and apparently have a less systematic relationship to human affective states than neuroendocrinological measures do.

For almost two decades, much effort and money have been spent in pursuit of peripheral psychochemical gauges in man. Because hospitalization of experimental subjects is necessary to control sample collection and to avoid dietary artifacts, the cost/effectiveness ratio of this approach must be viewed with reservations. If there has been a blind alley as we track the biochemical mechanisms underlying behavior, it has been the assumption that peripheral fluids relate to brain function in a simple or direct way. In the labyrinth in which we are working even empirical relationships are subject to much chance variation, and we should be skeptical of locating the exit from the maze by their lights alone. Peripheral determinations generally are not yielding a great deal of information. There are two possible exceptions, however. One is the hormonal work of Prange's and Kastin's groups, mentioned above, and the pituitary hormone work of Sachar et al. (1971).

The other is peripheral measurement of the enzymes involved in the biosynthesis of neurotransmitters. Anxiety and other reactions to stress have been associated with an increase of plasma dopamines-β-hydroxylase (DBH), probably from activation of the sympathetic nerves and the adrenal medulla with resulting secretion of intravesicular material into the plasma (Lovenberg et al., 1974; Goldstein et al. 1974). DBH, first characterized as a secretory passenger by Kirshner and Viveros (1972), may be a new and useful peripheral indicator of affective state. Choline acetyltransferase can be measured in CSF and is reduced by drugs that reduce anxiety and fear (Rimon et al., 1974). Platelet and red cell neurotransmitter enzymatic defects have been associated with affective disorder and with schizophrenia (Bunney et al., 1970; Murphy and Wyatt, 1972).

In contrast to metabolites measured in urine and plasma, levels of neurotransmitter metabolites in CSF have been meaningfully linked with depression and other psychiatric disturbances. The use of probenecid for kinetic analysis of amine turnover in CSF in psychiatric patients has been especially helpful in such studies (Goodwin et al., 1973). Investigators at NIMH, for example, have demonstrated that lithium markedly reduces biogenic amine metabolites in CSF, particularly 5-hydroxyindoleacetic acid, the end product of serotonin metabolism (Goodwin et al., 1975).

Chemically oriented psychiatric researchers understandably have studied the fluids available to them—urine, blood, CSF. But now we are developing neuropharmacological tools with which to manipulate and study brain tissue directly. Important contributions to the central neurochemistry of emotional states have not come from particular landmark studies; they have coalesced from work in several fields. Sparked by the leadership of Seymour Kety, the association of neurochemical measures with subjective states in man by means of neuropharmacological agents and operational definitions of animal behavior has become a recognized scientific paradigm.

The logic exploits the data as follows: Drug A produces neurochemical change B in an animal brain region comparable to a human brain region (midbrain, hippocampus, striate cortex, hypothalamus). Drug A produces behavior C in an experimental animal. Behavior C is a characteristic response to drugs of class C which produce behavior D in man. In studies correlating objective and subjective instruments with various classes of psychotropic drugs, behavior D is associated with a predominant subjective state E. The inference that subjective state E may have chemical change B as its neurochemical substrate calls for studies addressed to certain collateral questions. If environmental manipulation (sensory isolation, floor shock) produces behavior C, is neurochemical change B a necessary concomitant? Does a drug that produces human subjective state E produce behavioral change C and neurochemical change B in animals? Does an agent shown to produce neurochemical change B prove to be useful in treating an abnormal amount of E in man? Thus converge the fields of biochemistry, neurochemistry, neurobiology, neuropharmacology, psychopharmacology, and biological psychiatry, and the A to E research logic prevails today in multidisciplinary studies the world over.

Brodie and Shore (1957) first explored the unmapped territory of central biogenic amine mechanisms, drug action, and behavior. Since then there has been an historical progression of theoretical models with which we have tried to approach an understanding of central neurotransmitter function.

First, consider the bucket. What can a bucket do? It can be filled; it can hold something in storage; it can be emptied. In the mid-1950s researchers can be said to have operated with the bucket as their model. They measured the amines in the brain and how their levels were affected by the major psychoactive drugs at the time, reserpine and monoamine oxidase inhibitors. Reserpine depleted the stores of amines (norepinephrine, dopamine, serotonin) in the brain and depressed mood in humans and behavior in animals. On the other hand, iproniazid inhibited monoamine oxidase, compromising a major route of amine degradation, and elevated mood in man and increased spontaneous exploratory behavior in animals. Thus it seemed psychic energy and motor activity rose and fell with the amount in the bucket—simple hydrodynamics.

This biological notion of increases and decreases in amount had its parallel in psychodynamic theory, of course. We're not very advanced in American psychiatry today beyond the original Freudian theory of libido. If your bucket gets too full it turns sour—energy becomes anxiety. If you have the "right" amount of whatever it is you need, all is well.

But it's hard to think of the brain in such passive terms. A bucket doesn't *do* anything—it's only done to. The oversimplification became obvious about 1960, when some effective psychotropic drugs were found not to have any effect on the amount (levels) or amines in the bucket (brain). Tricyclic antidepressants worked better for depression than monoamine oxidase inhibitors, but the amine levels were the same before and after treatment. Perhaps the *functional* level of neurotransmitter was more relevant than the total level. Maybe what should have been measured was the rate at which the information was passing from one cell to another.

Now consider the train as a model. What does a train do? It carries something from one place to another. An amino acid precursor is converted to neurotransmitter and later metabolically destroyed, and on cross section, at any particular point in time and space, you'll see only one car of that train, whether the train is moving at 100 miles an hour or one mile an hour.

The critical measure then, in the train model, is the rate of transmitter turnover, and there are several ways that can be measured: 1) You can put in a radioactive amino acid and watch how fast it is turned into a transmitter. 2) You can put in a radioactive transmitter and watch how fast it disappears. 3) You can inhibit the metabolic degradation and see how quickly the transmitter piles up in front of the blockade. 4) You can block the exit of the metabolic acids and watch how fast they accumulate.

However, in order for any one of these measures to reflect the overall rate of turnover, you have to make the assumption that you are dealing with a steady state. That premise is essential to turnover technology, but, at the same time, the element of passivity it carries weakens the argument.

Yet the more of this work we do, the more we realize that drug and brain together change over time. The brain is gradually changing against the drug and, therefore, the drug is acting in a different way over time, working against a changing substrate. When you deal with turnover you can't operate without the idea of a steady state. Unfortunately your conclusions will suffer from the dualism that we face almost wherever we look at the biology of behavior. Before, "more" was up and "less" was down; now, "fast" is up and "slow" is down, whether we're talking about energy or mood.

Current psychopharmacological theory would have it that the major primary effect of the psychoactive drugs is to alter subcellular mobility of the amines. In neurotransmission there is release and reuptake of amine by the presynaptic nerve ending, and tricyclics block that reuptake. Phenothiazines alter access to the receptors. Amphetamines increase the rate of release and block reuptake. Cocaine increases the rate of release. According to the train model, the latency of these actions is short; the drugs do these things right away. The duration of the effect is short too; when the drug is not present the effect is gone.

The progression of these theoretical models parallels the accrual of any biochemical knowledge, really. The bucket model came into vogue with the discoveries of the presence of transmitter substances in brain tissue; the train model was conceived along with the elucidation of the pathways of synthesis and degradation of the amines. If you don't mind mixing metaphors you might conceive of running the train *through* the bucket. Some people do conceive matters that way, but to me that amounts to countering the unlikely implication that the bucket's supply can be utterly exhausted with the equally unlikely implication of a steady state and an infinite supply.

In attempts to graft onto the turnover model some understanding of the regulation of the pathways, because some of the data simply do not fit the steady state assumption, two feedback loops have been propounded: an electrophysiological one and a neurochemical one. There is evidence from which to infer a reciprocal relationship between postsynaptic impingement and presynaptic neuronal firing rate. For instance, when serotonergic transmission is facilitated, say with LSD, spontaneous unit firing rates monitored by microelectrodes in serotonergic cell bodies suddenly become silent (Foote et al., 1969). If dopaminergic transmission is blocked, say with haloperidol, there is a marked, immediate increase in the firing rate of dopaminergic cell bodies (Bunney et al., 1973). Biochemists have believed for years that, in the adrenergic systems at least, the rate-limiting enzyme in the synthesis of transmitter is inhibited by the product through competition for cofactor or some other means. For example, the norepinephrine present in the nerve ending can turn off the enzyme that has been filling the bucket. By this product-feedback inhibition model, when the nerve ending is depleted of norepinephrine there is a loss of inhibition and a consequent increase in the activity of tyrosine hydroxylase. Both these regulatory mechanisms manifest short latency and short duration, i.e. the effects are prompt and the presence of the drug is required.

The next paradigmatic crisis rears its head. Five minutes after injecting an animal with a tricyclic drug the reuptake of norepinephrine is blocked, depleting temporarily the amine stores in the synaptosomes and decreasing the product-feedback inhibition of the synthesizing enzyme, which, activated, produces more norepinephrine for release. All very neat, but it takes four weeks for tricyclics to be effectively antidepressant! Lithium also does its thing in the laboratory in half an hour, yet it is effective against mania in five or six days, often taking a year or more to be symmetrically prophylactic in manic-depressive psychosis. Even phenothiazines, which make a patient somnolent and lethargic immediately, will not change the mentation of a schizophrenic patient for a week or more; only gradually will the secondary symptoms of psychosis disappear. Moreover, all the psychotropic agents we use (except minor tranquilizers like diazepam or meprobamate) have another interesting characteristic: little or no tolerance develops to their use.

The initial, obvious explanation for the delayed efficacy of these drugs was that it takes a long time to get the appropriate level in the body. That was rational; we start people on low doses because of the side effects. But the side effects disappear relatively quickly, within a few days, and still the primary effect is delayed. Moreover, it has been shown in studies with large patient populations that higher doses do not necessarily increase the rate of remission; doubling or tripling the dose of imipramine over 150 mg a day has no effect on the onset of remission of depressive symptoms. In addition, when the drug is withdrawn from a depressive patient, his symptoms do not return for two or three weeks.

Now we need a model involving long time constants, and we have begun to look away from easily synthesized, rapidly metabolized molecules toward larger molecules with relatively longer half lives and toward the neural apparatus itself to find another feedback loop. In our department at UCSD we discern several possibly relevant processes in central synapses of the dopaminergic, noradrenergic, and serotonergic systems.

1) Receptor function. When normal transmitter-receptor interaction is decreased, receptors appear capable of compensatory alterations in sensitivity. Three weeks after destroying the catecholamine nerve endings with 6-hydroxydopamine, David Segal and Mark Geyer infused low volumes of norepinephrine to the brains of freely moving rats, potentiating their behavior (Geyer and Segal, 1973; Segal et al., 1974a). Since 6-hydroxydopamine also destroys the reuptake mechanism, the possibility that a loss of transmitter inactivation had caused the hyperactivity had to be ruled out. These investigators therefore pretreated with desmethylimipramine, which inhibits reuptake, infused the rats with low volumes of norepinephrine, and found the response not potentiated. Finally, they infused transmitter to the brains of rats that had received chronic treatment with α-methyl-p-tyrosine, which inhibits catecholamine synthesis; the behavioral response was potentiated. Apparently depletion of catecholamine levels in the synapse results in potentiated receptor sensitivity to the transmitters.

Some other hints are emerging with regard to receptor adaptability. If you treat with quantities of thorazine, which blocks norepinephrine receptors, and then test with amphetamine after stopping thorazine, the animal is supersensitive to amphetamine. Recently David Segal has shown that an injection of amphetamine sensitizes a rat to the drug, and the effects are measurable in behavioral terms after a second injection as long as three or four weeks later (Segal, 1975).

You may see similar phenomena in your clinical practice. If you stop psychotropic agents suddenly, particularly phenothiazines, after a time you may get an explosive emergence of the patient's psychosis. There is a haunting refrain from alcoholics and of people working with them for which we do not yet have hard data. They claim that sensitivity to alcohol is progressive even when an alcoholic is not drinking. Please don't ignore the alcoholic patient who describes progressive sensitivity; that phenomenon alone makes social drinking impossible for him. The idea of "practice" drinking or of a genetically vulnerable patient "learning" to drink is bizarre and irresponsible; I am always suspicious of six-month or one-year studies on a 30-year disease. The time constant in a study should approximate in some reasonable way the time constant of the disease. In sum, on the one hand receptors appear to adapt, but there may also be some kind of mechanism for sensitization, and it may not even be tied to postsynaptic receptors; it may be presynaptic.

2) Regulation of transmitter synthesizing enzymes in the nerve ending. Maintaining the integrity of synaptosomes, we can study the rate of conversion of substance to transmitter as a function of the physical state of the rate-limiting enzyme. Some drugs promptly alter enzyme activity in nerve endings. Amphetamine, for instance, can shift tyrosine hydroxylase activity from the soluble to the synaptosomal fraction and reduce the conversion of tyrosine to catecholamines at the same time. At 5 mg/kg the shift and the reduction occur within 30 minutes and last about six hours (Mandell et al., 1972). There is a clinical entity—post-amphetamine depression—with a comparable time constant; it used to be thought of as the result of exhaustion of catecholamine stores. Manipulating the divalent cations in the incubation medium, Ron Kuczenski has examined the effect of membrane binding on soluble tyrosine hydroxylase, and found the enzyme activity can be either activated or occluded by binding (Kuczenski and Mandell, 1972; Kuczenski, 1973a, 1973b). In the serotonergic system we have shown that the calcium ion activates tryptophan hydroxylase, and it is possible that there is some relationship between this and the

calcium influx associated with membrane depolarization upon electrical stimulation (Knapp et al., 1975).

3) Substrate uptake mechanisms. It appears that norepinephrine and dopamine synthesis are not limited by tyrosine supply. There is plenty of precursor in catecholamine nerve endings, but in the serotonergic system the biosynthetic mechanism may be unsaturated in the nerve ending, and therefore dependent on substrate uptake. Morphine inhibits intrasynaptosomal tryptophan hydroxylase activity without altering the rate of substrate uptake, but a number of other drugs do alter tryptophan uptake into the nerve endings (Knapp and Mandell, 1972a). The kinetics of tryptophan uptake into septal synaptosomes indicate that there are both low and high affinity uptake systems, and the latter, which is more sensitive to drugs, appears to be energy-dependent and stereo-specific. Lithium increases serotonin synthesis in striatal synaptosomes by stimulating the high affinity uptake of tryptophan (Knapp and Mandell, 1973, 1975); cocaine decreases serotonin synthesis by inhibiting the high affinity uptake (Knapp and Mandell, 1972a); neither affect the low affinity uptake. Still, the relationship between substrate uptake and conversion to transmitter in the serotonergic system is not well understood. However, tryptophan administration can make people sleepy and give them a sense of fullness, and there is evidence that tryptophan intake increases serotonin production by increasing uptake of precursor. Similarly, an anorectic called fenfluramine, a unique amphetamine, increases serotonin synthesis, and unlike any other anorectic agent, produces somnolence as well as a sense of fullness.

4) Delayed alterations in enzyme activity or amount. Changes induced in transmitter dynamics at the nerve ending somehow affect the rate of enzyme synthesis in the cell bodies, and those changes in amount of enzyme are seen later at the nerve endings. Chronic reserpine administration increases tyro-

sine hydroxylase activity in various areas of rat brain within nine days (Segal et al., 1971). Chronic administration of amphetamine or monoamine oxidase inhibitors decreases midbrain tyrosine hydroxylase activity. Morphine initially inhibits enzymatic activity in serotonergic synaptosomes, but immediately thereafter an increase in enzymatic activity appears in cell body regions; the increase is later seen at the nerve ending (Knapp and Mandell, 1972a). Lithium initially augments tryptophan uptake into synaptosomes and conversion of tryptophan to serotonin in nerve endings. This is associated with an almost immediate decrease in midbrain enzymatic activity, which decrease "arrives" at serotonergic nerve endings two weeks later (Knapp and Mandell, 1973, 1975). The latency between alterations in the enzymatic activity in cell body and nerve ending regions suggests that decreased or increased enzyme is moving by axoplasmic flow. When we inhibited tryptophan hydroxylase with parachlorophenylalanine and followed the defective enzyme activity as it moved from the midbrain to the septum, the rate of flow was calculable at about 1 to 2 mm per day or "slow flow" (Knapp and Mandell, 1972b).

The latency to action of some psychotropic drugs and the time required for the development of tolerance to addictive drugs as well as the traumata of withdrawal might be functions of this inevitable delay in macromolecular adjustment. For example, when a narcotics addict stops taking his drug, 12 to 18 hours pass before physiological withdrawal symptoms begin. They get severe at around two or three days; they reach a peak by five days. The addict is sweating and vomiting; he has muscle cramps and multiple erections and spontaneous ejaculations; he is incredibly hungry. It is as if all his neurological systems are GO. Gradually the symptoms subside. Then, between 10 and 12 days later they are suddenly exacerbated and may continue for another week. That second phase used to be called the psychological withdrawal, but I find myself imagining an asynchronous reversal of these adaptive mechanisms. It may take three or four days for the receptor function to return to baseline. Because opiates appear to block the erotonergic system, perhaps the second seige of symptoms has to do with how long it takes to reduce the enzyme that overcame the blockade.

Of course, with regard to the therapeutic efficacy of the psychotropic drugs, the *piece de resistance* of this speculative argument is the possibility that the treatments work by provoking the adaptation, or by invoking an extension of an endogenous adaptation. For example, to construct a model of affective disorder that incorporates the growing body of biochemical data from chronic drug studies as well as recent CSF metabolite findings in depressed patients, we could assume, contrary to the current theories, that the depression-prone patient has catecholamine receptors with heightened responsiveness (Segal et al., 1974b). Such a patient would manifest exaggerated reactions to stimuli that release biogenic amines and a consequent feedback-regulated decrease in presynaptic neuronal activity. If persistent, that compensatory decrease in presynaptic neuronal firing rate would result in less tyrosine hydroxylase being produced in the cell body and ultimately less enzyme functioning in the nerve ending. Depressed patients have been shown to have low amine metabolites in their CSF, reflecting decreased synthesis of catecholamines (Goodwin et al., 1973). Then chronic administration of a tricyclic antidepressant drug (blocking reuptake of the amines) would temporarily *increase* bombardment of the hyper-responsive receptor, leading subsequently to a further decrease in presynaptic firing rate. Goodwin et al. (1975) have found still lower levels of some amine metabolites in the CSF of depressed patients after treatment with tricyclics.

Very well, why doesn't further adaptive change to a pathologically responsive receptor occur naturally? Conceivably, inadequate adaptation reflects a defect in the compensatory apparatus itself. Moreover, Goldstein (1972) has shown that adaptive changes to such agents as morphine require, in addition to adequate dose, *persistence* of the stimulus. For example, tolerance develops much faster to maintained levels of morphine in the blood than to intermittently high levels. Whereas, without intervention, receptor activation by endogenous transmitters is likely to vary, tricyclic treatment produces a persistent increment. Could further compensatory adaptation resembling a tricyclic effect be produced by other kinds of intervention? Perhaps it could, if exaggerated synthesis, release, and persistent receptor bombardment by catecholamines could be achieved; perhaps the antidepressant effects of regular exercise or of repeated heat stress from daily saunas are achieved this way.

Descending from the rarified atmosphere of theoretical speculation, we are nevertheless left with the possibility that the fragments of neurobiological adaptation we are measuring today will emerge as prototypic of the mechanisms that serve a variety of neurotransmitter systems in the brain, and that through them we will better apprehend the complex symphony of psychopathology and adaptation in man.

REFERENCES

ARMSTRONG, M. D., SHAW, K. N., and WALL, P. E.: The phenolic acids of human urine; paper chromatography of phenolic acids. *J. Biol. Chem.*, 218:293-303, 1956.

AXELROD, J.: Metabolism of epinephrine and other sympathomimetic amines. *Physiol. Rev.*, 39:751-776, 1959.

BRODIE, B. B. and SHORE, P. A.: A concept for a role of serotonin and norepinephrine as chemical mediators in the brain. *Ann. N. Y. Acad. Sci.*, 66:631, 1957.

BUNNEY, B. S., WALTERS, J. R., ROTH, R. H., and AGHAJANIAN, G. K.: Dopaminergic neurons: Effect of antipsychotic drugs and amphetamine on single cell activity. *J. Pharmacol. Exp. Ther.*, 158:560-571, 1973.

BUNNEY, W. E., BRODIE, H. K. H., MURPHY, D. L., and GOODWIN, F. K.: Psychopharmacological differentiation between two subgroups of depressed patients. *Proc. Am. Psychol. Assn.*, 829-830, 1970.

ELMADJIAN, F.: Aldosterone excretion in behavioral disorders. *Res. Publ. Ass. Res. Nerv. Ment. Dis.*, 40:414-419, 1962.

FOOTE, W. E., SHEARD, M. H., and AGHAJIAN, G. K.: Comparison of effects of LSD and amphetamine on midbrain raphe units. *Nature*, 222:567-569, 1969.

GEYER, M. A. and SEGAL, D. S.: Differential effects of reserpine and alpha-methyl-p-tyrosine or norepinephrine and dopamine induced behavioral activity. *Psychopharmacologia*, 29:131-140, 1973.

GOLDSTEIN, A.: The pharmacologic basis of methadone treatment. *Proc. 4th Na. Conf. Methadone Treatment*, Nat. Assn. for the Prevention of Addiction to Narcotics (NAPAN), New York, 1972, pp. 27-32.

GOLDSTEIN, M., FREEDMAN, L. S., EBSTEIN, R. P., PARK, D. H., and KASHIMOTO, T.: Human serum dopamine-β-hydroxylase: Relationship to sympathetic activity in physiological and pathological states. *Psychopharmacol. Bulletin*, 10:25, 1974.

GOODWIN, F., POST, R., DUNNER, D., and GORDON, E.: Cerebrospinal fluid amine metabolites in affective illness: The probenecid technique. *Am. J. Psychiat.*, 130:73-79, 1973.

GOODWIN, F. K., SACK, R. L., and POST, R. M.: Clinical evidence for neurotransmitter adaptation in response to antidepressant therapy. In A. J. Mandell (Ed.): *Neurobiological Mechanisms of Adaptation and Behavior*. New York: Raven Press, 1975.

KASTIN, A. J., SCHALCH, D. S., EHRINSING, R. H., and ANDERSON, M. S.: Improvement in mental depression with decreased thyrotropin response after administration of thyrotropin-releasing hormone. *Lancet*, 2:740-742, 1972.

KIRSHNER, N. and VIVEROS, O.: The secretory cycle in the adrenal medulla. *Pharmacol. Rev.*, 24:385-398, 1972.

KNAPP, S. and MANDELL, A. J.: The effects of narcotic drugs on the brain's serotonin biosynthetic systems. *Science*, 177:1209-1211, 1972a.

KNAPP, S. and MANDELL, A. J.: Parachlorophenylalanine: Its three phase sequence of interactions with the two forms of brain tryptophan hydroxylase. *Life Sci.*, 2(16):761-771, 1972b.

KNAPP, S. and MANDELL, A. J.: Short- and long-term lithium administration: Effects on the brain's serotonergic biosynthetic systems. *Science*, 180:645-647, 1973.

KNAPP, S. and MANDELL, A. J.: Effects of lithium chloride on parameters of biosynthetic capacity for 5-hydroxytryptamine in rat brain. *J. Pharmacol. Exp. Ther.*, 193 (in press), 1975.

KNAPP, S., MANDELL, A. J., and BULLARD, W. P.: Calcium activation of brain tryptophan hydroxylase. *Life Sci.*, 16(9), in press, 1975.

KOPIN, I. J. and GORDON, E. K.: Metabolism of norepinephrine-H³ released by tyramine and reserpine. *J. Pharmacol. Exp. Ther.*, 138: 351-359, 1962.

KOPIN, I. J. and GORDON, E. K.: Metabolism of administered and drug-released norepinephrine-7-H^3 in the rat. *J. Pharmacol. Exp. Ther.*, 140:207-216, 1963.

KUCZENSKI, R.: Striatal tyrosine hydroxylases with high and low affinity for tyrosine: Implications for the multiple-pool concept of catecholamines. *Life Sci.*, 13:247-255, 1973a.

KUCZENSKI, R.: Soluble, membrane-bound, and detergent-solubilized rat striatal tyrosine hydroxylase: pH dependent cofactor binding. *J. Biol. Chem.*, 248:5074-5080, 1973b.

KUCZENSKI, R. T. and MANDELL, A. J.: Regulatory properties of soluble and particulate rat brain tyrosine hydroxylase. *J. Biol. Chem.*, 247:3114-3122, 1972.

LOVENBERG, W., BRUCKWICK, E. A., and ALEXANDER, R. W.: Evaluation of serum dopamine-β-hydroxylase activity as an index of sympathetic nervous activity in man. *Psychopharmacol. Bulletin*, 10:26-27, 1974.

MAAS, J. W. and LANDIS, D. H.: A technique for assaying the kinetics of norepinephrine metabolism in the central nervous system *in vivo*. *Psychosomat. Med.*, 28:247-256, 1966.

MAAS, J. W. and LANDIS, D. H.: *In vivo* studies of the metabolism of norepinephrine in the central nervous system. *J. Pharmacol. Exp. Ther.*, 163:147-162, 1968.

MANDELL, A. J., KNAPP, S., KUCZENSKI, R. T., and SEGAL, D. S.: Methamphetamine-induced alteration in the physical state of rat caudate tyrosine hydroxylase. *Biochem. Pharmacol.*, 21:2737-2750, 1972.

MURPHY, D. L. and WYATT, R. J.: Reduced monoamine oxidase activity in blood platelets from schizophrenic patients. *Nature*, 238:225-226, 1972.

PRANGE, A. J., WILSON, I. C., LARA, P. P., and ALLTOP, L. B.: Effects of thyrotropin-releasing hormone in depression. In A. J. Prange, Jr. (Ed.): *The Thyroid Axis, Drugs, and Behavior*. New York: Raven Press, 1974.

RIMON, R., MANDELL, A. J., PUHAKKA, P., and VANALAINEN, E.: Adrenergic blockade and cholinergic response in human cerebrospinal fluid. In N. S. Kline (Ed.): *Factors in Depression*. New York: Raven Press, 1974.

SACHAR, E. J., FINKELSTEIN, J., and HELLMAN, L.: Growth hormone responses in depressive illness. *Arch. Gen. Psychiat.*, 25:263-269, 1971.

SCHACHTER, S. and SINGER, J. E.: Cognitive, social, and physiological determinants of emotional state. *Psych. Rev.*, 69:379-399, 1962.

SCHILDKRAUT, J. J., GORDON, E. K., and DURELL, J.: Catecholamine metabolism in affective disorders. I. Normetanephrine and VMA excretion in depressed patients treated with imipramine. *J. Psychiat. Res.*, 3:213-228, 1965.

SEGAL, D. S.: Behavioral and neurochemical correlates of repeated d-amphetamine administration. In A. J. Mandell (Ed.): *Neuro-*

biological Mechanisms of Adaptation and Behavior. New York: Raven Press, 1975.

SEGAL, D. S., SULLIVAN, J. L., and MANDELL, A. J.: Effects of long-term reserpine on brain tyrosine hydroxylase and behavioral activity. *Science,* 173:847-849, 1971.

SEGAL, D. S., MCALLISTER, C., and GEYER, M. A.: Ventricular infusion of norepinephrine and amphetamine: direct versus indirect action. *Pharmacol. Biochem. Behav.,* 2:79-86, 1974a.

SEGAL, D. S., KUCZENSKI, R., and MANDELL, A. J.: Theoretical implications of drug-induced adaptive regulation for a biogenic amine hypothesis of affective disorder. *Biol. Psychiat.,* 9:147-159, 1974b.

4

Psychogenic Theories of Schizophrenia

Paul Chodoff, M.D.
and
William T. Carpenter, Jr., M.D.

In spite of the intense interest in schizophrenia manifested in clinical and scientific centers all over the world, it must be acknowledged that most of the problems about the description, classification and etiology of schizophrenia which puzzled the pioneers in the field are still with us and are largely unresolved. Although it is a strong statement, it seems true that for too long researchers have behaved as if their hypotheses account for schizophrenia and have not been sufficiently willing to recognize the severe limitations of every piece of work accomplished to date. In spite of pious protestations, most researchers tend to occupy positions which might be characterized as biophobe or psychophobe even though such a dichotomy is regularly denounced by representatives of both positions. In fact, there has been very little integration of biological and psychological data and theory. An important reason for this is that the data base for research in schizophrenia constitutes too narrow a foundation for the wide range of exploration built upon it. Claims which purport to account for schizophrenia are too often based on findings in a few patients (perhaps schizophrenic) which may—or more probably may not—be replicated, which may—or more probably may not—be discriminating, and whose explanatory power depends more on the ambitious theoretical framework in which the claims are set than on the findings themselves.

In the following summary and critical discussion of the current status of psychogenic theories of schizophrenia, theoretical and methodological difficulties will be apparent. However, because both biologically-oriented and psychologically-oriented research are similarly limited by major methodologic problems, we introduce our paper with a brief discussion of some factors which critically restrict the interpretation of data and evaluation of hypotheses about schizophrenia, no matter what their source:

1. The lack of reliability of the diagnosis of schizophrenia.
2. Schizophrenia may not be a single entity, but rather multiple illnesses, each of which may be the result of multiple etiologic factors.
3. The possibly significant differences between acute and chronic schizophrenia.
4. The position of the observer.

1. Lack of diagnostic reliability is a perennial problem in psychiatry (1-4) and is not confined to schizophrenia. However, a combination of inadequate or improperly utilized diagnostic tools, the absence of validating criteria, and the lack of a sophisticated interest in descriptive psychiatry has played havoc in schizophrenia research by calling into question the diagnosis of the subjects on whom the research has been performed. Since

Kraepelin, the diagnosis of schizophrenia has depended on presenting signs and symptoms. Although systems have been developed which make it possible to identify symptoms with a high discriminating value (5-9), these systems have been insufficiently employed by investigators, thus contributing to one of the most consistent and troublesome trends in schizophrenia research—the failure of replication attempts.

2. Whether schizophrenia is an illness, or a group of illnesses, or a syndrome has been debated since Kraepelin's concept of an illness, dementia praecox, was changed by Bleuler to the group of schizophrenias. The question is still not settled whether the differing although related conditions which now receive the diagnosis are all manifestations of the same underlying illness, or are a collection of overlapping but distinct diseases. The failure to resolve this issue has a stultifying effect on research in schizophrenia (10). The vast majority of reports in the literature appear to be based on relatively heterogeneous groups of subjects, with the result that potentially important findings are diluted and may be missed altogether. For instance, if a researcher includes both hebephrenic and catatonic patients in his sample, a finding applicable to the catatonics but irrelevant to the other sub-types will be attenuated. An investigator intrepid enough to seek "the" cause of schizophrenia is constantly frustrated by the fact that there is little reason to believe that a single etiology will ever be found for any sub-type of schizophrenia, and it is much more likely that the illness will be understood only by invoking a combination of genetic, biochemical, environmental and intrapsychic variables. To the extent that these variables differ in each sub-type of schizophrenia, heterogeneous patient cohorts will reduce the amount of variance accounted for by each factor and thus lessen chances of meaningful findings.

3. The significant differences between the entity known as chronic schizophrenia and that known as acute schizophrenia

have not fully been taken into account in schizophrenia research. Very compelling evidence is emerging that good pre-morbid, acute schizophrenic patients differ from poor pre-morbid, chronic patients, and that the differences are not related specifically to the phase of illness. The Danish adoptive studies provide strong evidence that patients identified as acute schizophrenics do not have biologic relatives with chronic schizophrenia or schizophrenia spectrum disease (11). These findings and others (12, 13, 14) suggest strongly that process or poor pre-morbid schizophrenia is more biologically bound than good pre-morbid, reactive, or acute schizophrenia, in which experiential factors may be more important. To the extent that researchers have chosen to study chronic patients, their findings have been complicated by the effects of institutionalization, of chronicity itself, and of particular dietary regimens and other artifacts. Often the findings of such studies are related less to the illness—schizophrenia—than to the living circumstances of the schizophrenic individual. Much psychoanalytic investigation has been undertaken in chronic hospitalized patients while family theorists have included among their subjects more young patients, including outpatients. Thus it can be inferred that the family findings, unlike those resulting from earlier psychoanalytic studies, are based on both reactive and process schizophrenic patients, although this characterization of the patients under study is not generally stated.

4. The vantage point from which observations are made surely will influence the data compiled by the investigator. Metabolic processes will not be illuminated by purely psychoanalytic researchers, nor will subtle communication defects be noted in the course of biochemical or epidemiologic studies. Evidence supporting a hypothesis in one area is seldom directly relevant to hypotheses from other areas. Thus, findings in biologic investigations, for example, rarely have confirming or refuting implications for a particular psychological hypothesis.

The same often applies for hypotheses put forward by investigators within the same general theoretical orientation.

If this general critique of research in schizophrenia is valid, then acceptance of investigative results will depend on how satisfactorily a particular study design answers the following questions: 1) What are the characteristics and distinguishing features of the patients under investigation? If it appears reasonable to regard them as schizophrenic, do they represent a heterogeneous sample or can a more specific subgroup be identified? Are they suffering from a chronic or an acute disturbance? 2) Does the manner in which the investigation is conducted generate data which have the potential of refuting the hypothesis? 3) If results of the investigation support an etiologic hypothesis, is it possible to estimate the amount of variance in manifest schizophrenia accounted for by the particular factor under consideration?

We turn now to an overview of the current state of the art with regard to primarily psychogenic theories of schizophrenia. Our scope is admittedly limited since we are surveying only results from psychoanalytic (broadly defined) investigations and those from family studies. We do not include findings derived from learning and behavioral theory, nor from studies with an epidemiologic or sociological perspective. We do not consider the hypothesis that schizophrenia is simply a pejorative label for the effects of a corrupt society on certain sensitive individuals, nor do we regard schizophrenia as a myth.

Possibly the most pertinent observation to be made about primarily psychodynamic theories of schizophrenia today is to contrast the current state of retrenchment and even defensiveness with the high-water mark during the post World War II period. A manifestation of this trend is the significant decline in the current psychiatric literature in articles dealing with the psychotherapy of schizophrenia (15). The burgeoning of interest in schizophrenia as a basically psychogenic disorder during the forties and fifties was the work of a new generation of psychoanalysts stimulated and optimistic about the possibilities of extending psychoanalytic research and treatment into unexplored realms, including even schizophrenia, in spite of Freud's cautionary dictum (16) about its imperviousness to psychoanalytic attack. The pioneering work of Harry Stack Sullivan (17) in this field was very influential, especially for the important group of psychoanalytic investigators of schizophrenia identified with Chestnut Lodge Sanitorium.* This decline in interest can be attributed to a number of factors. As the base of clinical psychiatry has broadened, and as new social and pharmacologic treatment methods have proven their effectiveness, the previous dominance of psychoanalysis has waned. The contrast between the apparent efficacy of drug treatment of schizophrenia and the arduous, difficult, costly and uncertain results of psychotherapy with schizophrenics has had a profound effect (18, 19, 20). However, serious problems in assessing course and outcome in schizophrenia have not been adequately dealt with to date, so that too much assurance about comparative treatment effects (21-24) is not yet justified. In addition, hard evidence has been demonstrated for the existence of a significant genetic factor in some schizophrenic subgroups (11). This finding has been interpreted as posing a challenge to advocates of the psychogenic view of schizophrenia even though the presence of constitutional factors has been at least formally acknowledged by such theorists as far back as Freud (25).

Current psychoanalytic contributors to schizophrenia are engaged in a lively debate between those who espouse what has been called a deficit theory of schizophrenia and the proponents of a conflict theory. Both camps can invoke the name of Freud in support of their arguments—early Freud for the conflict (16,

---

*These include Burnham, Fromm-Reichman, Kafka, Pao, Schultz, Searles, Stanton, and Hill as well as Sullivan himself.

26) and later Freud (25) for the deficit theory. These models have been ably summarized by Gunderson (27).

The deficit model postulates an early, severe deficit in the perceptual apparatus or central organizational learning capacity which prevents the pre-schizophrenic child from normal internalization of early parental experiences necessary to produce a stable sense of self. At times of later stress the schizophrenic is overwhelmed as these brittle internalizations fragment, leading to pathologic attempts to restore object relations and to the familiar phenomenology of schizophrenia. In this view (28) the symptoms of the illness have a coherence which reflects a deficit in internal organization manifested subjectively by a sense of internal catastrophe. This development is an outcome, not of intrapsychic conflict as in neurosis, but of a deficiency in important psychological functions necessary for growth, development and adaptation. Schizophrenia cannot be understood as a compromise resolution of conflict, but rather as the behavioral manifestations of some psychological deficit. This formulation harks back to Rado's concept (29) of the schizotype who decompensates under stress and becomes a schizophrenic.

The advocates of a conflict theory of schizophrenia, unlike proponents of a deficit model, postulate that the psychogenesis of schizophrenia stems from an early and severe intrapsychic conflict differing only in depth, severity, and mode of defense from the infantile conflicts predisposing to neurosis. While conflict theorists share this assumption, they vary widely in their attempts to account for the ontogenesis of schizophrenia. Two important variants of the conflict model, which will only be mentioned here, are: 1) the Kleinian approach where the predisposition to schizophrenia is found in what Klein has described as the paranoid-schizoid position in three- to six-month infants (30, 31), and 2) the ego psychological view that schizophrenia results from ego defects generated by defenses against anxiety as in the neuroses (32). However, the version of conflict theory known as the theory of affect intolerance lends itself more readily to integration with psychobiologic information, and thus will receive further mention.

Affect intolerance theory states that the pre-schizophrenic avoids relationships as a means of controlling the danger of developing intense and potentially intolerable affects. It is consistent with Sullivan's (17) concept of the malevolent transformation which takes place in the child who has regularly experienced rejection when tenderness or affection should have been forthcoming, and of Frieda Fromm-Reichman's (33) emphasis on the schizophrenic's dilemma of being barred by the danger of uncontrolled feelings from the intimacy for which he unconsciously longs. This way of looking at schizophrenia has been attractive to many clinicians since it seems to characterize the schizophrenic impasse more understandably than other formulations. Grinker (34), for instance, feels that the inability to experience anger is at the base of schizophrenic decompensation. It is an important element in the concept of the "need-fear dilemma" of Donald Burnham (35), which relates tenuous control of affect, of consciousness and thought, and of actions to weak internal structure, especially those systems involved in self-control and self-regulation. Burnham's work partially reconciles conflict and deficit theory. This is also true of Aronson's (36) revision of deficit theory which gives increased emphasis to the strength rather than the weakness of the vulnerable infant's learned responses to frustration. He recognizes, however, that these responses become maladaptive when confronted with other demands of life.

Ping-Nie Pao (37) has recently provided a general theory of schizophrenia including both conflict and deficit elements. He is one of many psychoanalytic investigators who uses Margaret Mahler's (38) formulation of a symbiotic theory of infantile psychosis. Mahler sees faulty mutual cueing between infant and mother due to whatever cause (constitutional defect and/or inadequate mothering) as potentially responsible for either infantile or adult psychosis. Pao elaborates and enriches this model by applying the work of a number of psychoanalytic theorists and observers of infantile behavior. He also asserts that it offers a rationale—the concept of "corrective symbiotic experience"—for long-term intensive treatment of schizophrenic patients.

The deficit and conflict theories both have their strengths and weaknesses, some aspects of which have recently been debated (39). The deficit model has the major advantage of allowing for a probably genetic defect which can become the necessary if not sufficient cause for the later development of a psychosis. It is also true that accepting the deficit model limits the role of psychological factors to the way the inborn defect interacts with environmental elements to produce the schizophrenic illness. A deficit theory, therefore, does not attempt a complete etiologic formulation of schizophrenia on a psychogenic basis and thus may have a limiting effect on psychotherapeutic endeavors with schizophrenic patients. Some of its proponents believe that the standard psychoanalytic procedure is not only inappropriate but actually dangerous (40). For them, "the principal psychotherapeutic effort is aimed at making and keeping contact, struggling to insure communication and fostering identification with a caring and concerned therapist" (28). However, a therapist who believes that his patient suffers from a defect which even theoretically cannot be altered inevitably will have a different perspective towards his patient's problems than a therapist who is convinced that his patient's suffering results from non-genetic internal conflict. That the former attitude may constitute a danger to the therapeutic relationship has been pointed out in Harold Searles's (41) warning that deficit theory might "set schizophrenic persons apart qualitatively and indelibly from their fellow human beings as in their very essence something less than human." Put in another way it may make it more difficult for therapists to adhere to Sullivan's profound but simple aphorism that "we are all more simply human than otherwise." More subtle interferences with psychotherapeutic work stemming from belief in, or at least ambivalence about, the presence of a genetic component may have an effect on the attitudes and counter-transference of a therapist who feels doubtful or defensive about the value of the psychotherapeutic approach, and who may wonder whether he is engaged in an unreal, quixotic endeavor (42). If this results in an over-identification with the patient, the therapist may be reluctant to prescribe indicated drugs because this means that he is giving up and abandoning his patient. On the other hand, acceptance of the role of an inborn factor may relieve the therapist from a sense of failure if his results are not as thoroughgoing as he would wish.

Conflict theories, unlike the deficit models, permit an ambitious approach to the psychotherapy of schizophrenic patients, including even the classical psychoanalytic approach. Also, they can be thought of as attempting to provide a more complete model of the psychogenesis of schizophrenia than is possible for deficit theories. However, conflict theories must rise or fall depending on whether the various elements which compose them can be brought together in a coherent and cohesive fashion, whether the retrospective reconstructions of early mother-child relationships can be validated by other methods such as prospective studies, whether the psychodynamic formulations advanced to explain vulnerability to schizophrenia can be differentiated from such patterns said to underlie other psychopathological conditions and, finally, whether the conflict theories can bear fruit in a consistent way in psychotherapeutic results. Thus far, data relevant to these conditions do not clearly confirm or refute the basic tenets of conflict theory.

Whatever their differences, both conflict and deficit theories of schizophrenia, as well as the attempts to synthesize them, are derived primarily from psychoanalytic observation and inference. They are concerned primarily with the nature and quality of a child's early object relationships. A current and active worker in this tradition is Silvano Arieti, whose recent second edition of *Interpretation of Schizophrenia* (43) provides a thoroughgoing exposition of the psychogenic view. Arieti sees the development of schizophrenia as beginning in early childhood when the future patient is exposed to an abnormal interpersonal environment, generally dominated by the influence of the mother. This is the origin of the primary schizophrenic cleavage between the malevolent "Thou" and the "Bad Me." In late childhood, the response to this abnormal childhood environment itself becomes abnormal, and the child comes to see himself as weak and ineffectual. This negative self-image develops further in adolescence and is projected onto what is then experienced as a hostile outside world. However, the actual onset of a psychosis comes about only when the cognitive functions undergo a profound alteration through the work, in other words, of the schizophrenic thought disorder.

Here Arieti comes to grips with the nature and origin of the peculiar style of cognition which has been considered to be the hallmark of schizophrenia since the time of Bleuler. It has always been a subject of great interest to investigators of schizophrenia who have undertaken to explain it in various ways. Wynne and Singer (44-47), particularly concerned with the disturbed communicative patterns in families of schizophrenics, concluded that these patterns were familial characteristics and that the amorphous and fragmented styles of thinking of psychotic schizophrenics were learned in the family context. Lidz (48) has labeled the thought disorder "egocentric overinclusiveness." He believes that "the parent's disturbed styles of communication which are manifestations of their egocentricities are essential precursors of the patient's cognitive regression that occurs when he cannot surmount the essential development task of adolescence." Arieti (15) proposes that the schizophrenic thought disorder constitutes a regression to what he calls primary process cognition which has a structure of its own, paleological rather than logical. He emphasizes that without this transformation of thought processes there can be no psychosis, regardless of the abnormal and traumatic nature of the childhood experiences. Irrationality is not transmitted directly. Intervening between the pathological child-family complex and the psychosis there must occur the restructuring manifested by the thought disorder.

The predilection for concrete thinking and the apparent inability to operate on a conceptual or metaphorical level are characteristic of the schizophrenic thinking disorder. Searles (49) regards this as a defense which protects against the incursion into consciousness of certain affects, rather than as a more or less fixed and unalterable quality intrinsic to the psychic and cognitive organization of schizophrenia. This view is consistent with a more hopeful psychotherapeutic approach.

It is clear that these other explanations of the schizophrenic thought disorder from the psychodynamic and psychogenic points of view differ from each other in important respects, and do not provide an entirely coherent and generally accepted explanation of it. Yet, they do represent serious attempts to understand a phenomenon which is basic to schizophrenia. Specific attention to the schizophrenic thinking disorder has not been prominent among those who advance an organic or biological model, even though this style of thinking disorder does not resemble that seen in known organic psychosyndromes.

Psychoanalytically based observers have focused their attention primarily on the early object relationships of the future patient, particularly with his mother. In stark contrast to the mythology of the "American apple pie mom," the schizophrenogenic mother emerged as a malevolent figure whose inhumanity, both gross and subtle, rendered her child incapable of separating and individuating from a common symbiotic matrix. A prominent feature in current thinking about the development of schizophrenia has been a withdrawal from this formulation. Arieti in his recent (15) work expresses his belief that the influence of the mother, while obviously very important, has been exaggerated and distorted. The enormous emphasis on the mother's influence provided little attention to the personality of the child himself. He was seen as little more than an empty vessel being poisoned by maternal milk, rather than as an active agent contributing to his own fate. It is true that schizophrenics often describe their mothers in harsh terms, but Arieti suggests (15) that this relates to their undue sensitivity to the negative, and relative obliviousness to the positive, characteristics of their mothers. The negative reaction of the mother, in turn, would set up a vicious cycle of enmity between mother and child. The pathologic sensitivity of the child may be a genetically determined vulnerability. Arieti now views the mother of the pre-schizophrenic not as a monster, but more properly as a person overcome by the difficulties of living caused by an unhappy marriage, her own neurotic difficulties, and by the impact of the changing role of women with its destructive effects on the nuclear family. One might speculate that another reason for the unfavorable view of the mother, as expressed by schizophrenics in psychoanalytic psychotherapy, is the result of unconscious guiding by the therapist whose theory leads him to expect such an attitude. The recent exchange (50) between Arieti and Lidz in the *American Journal of Psychiatry* illustrates the strength of the current reaction against the concept of the malevolent schizophrenogenic mother. In a similar vein, Searles (41) states that in recent years he has come to be impressed by the role of the child itself in contributing to the failure of a loving mother-child relationship. He now sees the entire family as involved in a tragedy where all are overwhelmed and none are to blame. It is worth noting that Esca-

Iona (51), Mahler (52) and Bender (53) some years previously had already cautioned that the unusual attributes of the mothers of schizophrenics might well be the end result of years of attempting to relate to an abnormally developing child who, from earliest infancy, was less responsive to handling and caring than their other children. It is unfortunate that the early cautionary note sounded by these distinguished women has only recently been heeded in conceptualizing the mother-child interaction in schizophrenia.

Researchers using the family approach to schizophrenia are concerned with the nature of the transactions within the family which led to the development of the illness in the index case. They have particularly emphasized and studied the role of altered and distorted styles of communication in these families. Most of this work has been carried out by American investigators—Laing (54) is the best-known exception—using as a base Sullivan's interpersonal theory (17) and the work of cognitive theorists like von Domarus (55) and Vigotsky (56). Major contributions included the hypothesis of the double bind transaction (57, 58), the transmission of irrationality (48), concepts of pseudomutuality and pseudohostility (59) and the operationalized concepts of amorphous and fragmented communication styles in the parents of schizophrenics (44-47).

The intriguing Bateson-Jackson (57, 58) concept of the double bind seems to have suffered something of the fate of the malevolent schizophrenogenic mother who, incidentally, was generally expected to be the bearer of the double binding message. It has become clear that this mechanism operates in many psychopathological settings besides those productive of schizophrenia and, in addition, it may be compatible with health (60).

One of the recent additions to family theories of schizophrenia has been the work of Helm Stierlin, who has recently extended and refined the Wynne-Singer transactional modes (61). These are defined as the interplay of pushes and pulls occurring in families and affecting the individuation-separation process of offspring while operating as a covert organizing background for overt child-parent interactions. The major modes are defined as binding (the child is overprotected and the dependency bond held tight), expelling (the child is overtly rejected), and delegating. By the delegating mode is meant a pseudoencouragement for the child to separate from the parents so long as he is actually fulfilling covert parental missions. Although the modes are not necessarily pathogenic, a schizophrenic development may result from extreme degrees of the binding and delegating modes. The clinical manifestations are more severe and prognoses poorer in those illnesses arising from the former than from the latter. Patients from the delegating family mode are also more likely to be acutely rather than chronically disturbed as they attempt to carry out such impossible programs as destroying one parent out of loyalty to the other, embodying and actualizing grandiose parental ego ideals, and embodying and externalizing the craziness which the patient fears in himself. It is of interest that this description of the pathogenic effect of the delegating modes is similar not only to Wynne's concept of pseudomutuality (59), but also to the Lidz-Fleck description (48) of the skewed family structure which is productive of schizophrenia. This confluence of clinical observations suggests a considerable area of consensus about the schizophrenogenic potential of a family structure in which a facade of parental unity covers deep-seated dissonances and conflicting messages to the pre-schizophrenic child. However, reverting to the cautionary note which was sounded in the introduction to this paper, it is necessary to ask: Are these transactions essential to the development of schizophrenia? Are similar family patterns found in other psychological illnesses or in normals? Are they etiologic in schizophrenia, or the effect of the presence of a disturbed child?

In his recent book based on years of work in the field, Lidz

(48) postulates schizophrenia as primarily a psychogenic rather than an organic condition. He finds schizophrenia only in seriously disturbed families in which a global failure to permit adequate personality development in the child is caused by the transmission of the egocentricities and narcissistic needs of one or both parents to the child through the parents' disturbed style of communication. The child brought up in such a milieu is badly prepared for life and remains tied to the parental problems. He is thus unable to cope with the developmental task of achieving independence from his parents and of developing a strong self-identity and a capacity for intimacy. Faced with the stresses of adolescence the pre-schizophrenic's thinking becomes egocentrically overinclusive, and he falls back to earlier and more primitive forms of cognition earlier learned from his parents.

Although Lidz's claim (48) that family research has resulted in a comprehensive and satisfactory theory of the psychogenesis of schizophrenia without the need for postulating an organic-genetic component is questionable, the similarity in findings of a number of the groups working with schizophrenic families is remarkable. Furthermore, these data interdigitate comfortably with cognitive theory derived from individually based psychoanalytic exploration. A particularly cogent and convincing finding, and one which is not accounted for by those supporting an exclusive biogenetic position, is Singer's ability (62) consistently to identify the adoptive parents of schizophrenics by analyzing Rorschach test data. However, although promising, the work of the family theorists, like that of individual psychoanalytic workers, remains sub judice. The barriers to acceptance of a conflict theory of schizophrenia noted above must also be surmounted by family theorists if their approach to a psychological model of schizophrenia is to compete successfully with, or to be complementary to, genetic-organic models. Evidence for specificity of family transactions to schizophrenia are accruing and can be found elsewhere by the interested reader (47, 63, 64, 65).

It is not difficult to mount a critique of psychogenic theories of schizophrenia from the point of view of their conceptual and methodological inadequacies. There is the perennial problem, not unique to schizophrenia research, of the extent to which findings derived from psychoanalytical exploration of individual cases can be generalized. Referring back to the issues raised in the introductory section of this paper, it is clear that the work we have reviewed must still be regarded as preliminary. Clinical and nosological characteristics of the patients in psychogenic studies are too often inadequately described. Sampling bias is rarely dealt with, and limits to applicability of generalizations are not respected. Too frequently psychological data are dealt with as if pertaining to an exclusive universe without taking into account or attempting to integrate findings from other fields of inquiry. Hypotheses are rarely postulated so that refuting evidence can be brought to bear, or, in some cases, even imagined.

That these shortcomings in psychoanalytic and family investigations of schizophrenia are not unique is true, but not particularly to the point. Neither arrogance nor defensiveness are appropriate attitudes for workers in a field which is so extraordinarily difficult and complex as that of attempting to understand schizophrenia. In the closing portion of this paper we will advance some arguments favoring psychodynamic inquiry and treatment.

First, and probably most important, it is impossible to understand schizophrenia without taking into account the intrapsychic and interpersonal abnormalities of the individual manifesting the condition. No biogenetic theory pretends to fully account for the disturbed behavior of the schizophrenic (66). The etiologic relevance of psychogenic factors will undoubtedly vary enormously for different subgroups of schizophrenia, but there is no reason to consider them absent in any case. They may account for only certain aspects of the disordered behavior in cases with a heavy genetic vulnerability while being more fully responsible for the pathogenesis of other cases in which a genetic predisposition is less important.

Next, the vision of the psychoanalytic investigator may be narrow, but it is deep, and it is holistic in a way which is not true of workers who focus their attention solely on biologic variables. The method used in psychogenic inquiry is clinical observation, the backbone of modern scientific medicine. Furthermore, there is no necessary antagonism between this kind of investigation and a respectful adherence to the principles of science to the extent that they can be adapted to dealing with the complex behavior of human beings. This is illustrated, for instance, by the attention that Wynne-Singer (44-47) have given to classification, subject selection, comparative groups, double-blind methodologies and disprovable hypotheses.

It seems fair to ask if the several decades of investigation into the psychogenetic and psychodynamic factors has resulted in any consensus. We believe that such a consensus has been achieved about the following propositions: 1) Schizophrenia, or at least chronic schizophrenia, develops in a family milieu which is seriously disturbed. This disturbance may be gross and overt, but it also may be subtle in character and not immediately obvious to superficial observation. 2) Faulty and idiosyncratic communicative processes within the family are central to the family disturbance. 3) The early object relations of the future schizophrenic do not proceed in a healthy development, but are blighted in a way which has serious consequences for later adaptation. 4) The schizophrenic patient suffers an agonizing ambivalence in his attitude towards interpersonal closeness.

Finally, efforts to deal with schizophrenics therapeutically cannot proceed satisfactorily, whatever the principal mode of treatment, unless the therapist is able to understand the person with whom he is dealing. Simply to regard a schizophrenic patient as an ingester of phenothiazines strips him of his humanity, and countless numbers of patients are on drugs with little or no further therapeutic endeavor. As Cancro has put it (67), "the recognition of a genetic factor cannot and does not free us from the responsibility of knowing and relating to our patients in depth." Psychotherapeutic approaches to schizophrenics, ranging from clinical relationships which are complementary to other modes of treatment to the bold forays of a Searles or a Will, cannot proceed in a theoretical vacuum. Some frame of reference is necessary for the therapist to become involved in the seemingly chaotic world of the schizophrenic. The best foundations for such a frame of reference are supplied by the psychogenic theories we have outlined. In one sense, the veridical quality of theories on which one bases his contact with the schizophrenic is not the only index of their value. In dealing with madness, organizing principles are needed to permit a reasoned and human approach. Without the capacity to understand irrational behavior, man has regularly isolated and restrained the mad. This has been done with chains and chronic institutions, and may even be considered as one aspect of the situation today when millions of people are placed in chemical restraints, often to their benefit but sometimes as a result of an almost automatic reflex. Viewed in this light, the question of whether and to what extent psychotherapy is effective, although obviously very important, is not the only factor mandating its usage.

At the beginning of this paper we alluded to the diminished state of interest in the psychogenic approach to schizophrenia. We believe we have demonstrated, nonetheless, that significant research is progressing and that an important body of data has accumulated. Primary reasons for the decrease of interest in psychogenic and psychodynamic aspects of schizophrenia are the impact of the new genetic data and the high visibility of the effects of drug treatment as contrasted with the lack of documented evidence establishing the value of psychotherapy. For the psychogenic position to flourish, there will have to be a real, not just a lip service, acceptance of the multiplicity of etiological factors in schizophrenia. Workers from both biogenetic and psychogenetic areas must take seriously the findings of the other if better integrated theories are to evolve. From the psychogenic side there are some encouraging signs. We refer to prospective studies already under way involving high risk groups, which focus on interpersonal and intrapsychic phenomena but also take into account genetic loading, biochemical attributes, psychophysiological dispositions, nosological criteria and longitudinal assessment (68); to Arieti's suggestion (15) that the genetic component becomes manifest as undue sensitivity in the infant; and to Pao's (37) use of Freud's concept of the complementary series (constitutional and experiential) in his efforts to produce a unified theory. Efforts like these may be only faltering steps on the pathway towards a real synthesis, but they deserve to be taken seriously and to be matched with similar ecumenical steps by biogenetic investigators who must be mindful of the tremendous distance between a twisted gene and a twisted mind.

REFERENCES

1. BABIGIAN, H. M., GARDNER, E. H., MILES, H. C., and ROMANO, J.: Diagnostic consistency and change in a follow-up study of 1215 patients. *Am. J. Psychiatry*, 121:895, 1965.
2. COOPER, J. E., KENDELL, R. E., GURLAND, B. J., SHARPE, L., COPELAND, J. R. M., and SIMON, R.: *Psychiatric Diagnosis in New York and London—A Comparative Study of Mental Hospital Admissions*. London: Oxford University Press, 1972.
3. KATZ, M. M., COLE, J. O., and LOWERY, H. A.: Studies of the diagnostic process: The influence of symptom perception, past experience, and ethnic background on diagnostic decisions. *Am. J. Psychiatry*, 125:937, 1969.
4. KRAMER, M.: Cross-national study of diagnosis of the mental disorders: Origin of the problem. *Am. J. Psychiatry*, 125:1-11, April 1969 supplement.

5. ASTRACHAN, B. M., HARROW, M., ADLER, D., BRAUER, L., SCHWARTZ, A., SCHWARTZ, C., and TUCKER, G.: A checklist for the diagnosis of schizophrenia. *Br. J. Psychiatry*, 121:529-539, 1972.
6. CARPENTER, W. T., JR. and STRAUSS, J. S.: Cross-cultural evaluation of Schneider's first rank symptoms of schizophrenia: A report from the International Pilot Study of Schizophrenia. *Am. J. Psychiatry*, 131:682-687, 1974.
7. CARPENTER, W. T., JR., STRAUSS, J. S., and BARTKO, J. J.: A flexible system for the identification of schizophrenia: A report from the International Pilot Study of Schizophrenia. *Science*, 182:1275-1278, 1973.
8. FEIGHNER, J., ROBINS, E., GUSE, S., WOODRUFF, R., JR., WINOKUR, G., and MUNOZ, R.: Diagnostic criteria for use in psychiatric research. *Arch. Gen. Psychiatry*, 26:57-63, 1972.
9. World Health Organization: *The International Pilot Study of Schizophrenia*, vol. 1. Geneva: World Health Organization, 1973.
10. CARPENTER, W. T., JR.: Are there subtypes of schizophrenia? Presented at the Annual Meeting of the American Psychiatric Association, Detroit, Michigan, 1974.
11. KETY, S. S., ROSENTHAL, D., WENDER, P., ET AL.: The types and prevalency of mental illness in the biological and adoptive families of adoptive schizophrenics. In D. Rosenthal and S. S. Kety (Eds.): *The Transmission of Schizophrenia*. Oxford: Pergamon Press, 1968, pp. 345-362.
12. CARPENTER, W. T., JR., MURPHY, D. L., and WYATT, R. J.: Platelet monoamine oxidase activity in acute schizophrenia. *Am. J. Psychiatry*, 132:438-441, 1975.
13. GARMEZY, N.: Process and reactive schizophrenia: Some conceptions and issues. *Schizophrenia Bull.*, No 2, 1970, pp. 30-74.
14. GOLDSTEIN, M. J.: Premorbid adjustment, paranoid status, and patterns of response to phenothiazine in acute schizophrenia. *Schizophrenia Bull.*, No. 3, Winter 1970.
15. ARIETI, S.: An overview of schizophrenia from a predominantly psychological approach. *Am. J. Psychiatry*, 131(3):241-249, 1974.
16. FREUD, S.: *Neuropsychoses of Defense*. S.E., 3:41-68. London: Hogarth Press, 1953.
17. SULLIVAN, H. S.: *The Interpersonal Theory of Psychiatry*. New York: Norton, 1953.
18. GRINSPOON, L., EWALT, J. R., and SHADER, R.: Long-term treatment of chronic schizophrenia. *Int. J. Psychiatry*, 4(2):116-128, 1967.
19. HOGARTY, G. E., GOLDBERG, S. C., SCHOOLER, N. R., ULRICH, R. F., ET AL.: II. Two-year relapse rates. *Arch. Gen. Psychiatry*, 3(5):603-608, 1974.
20. MAY, P. R. A.: *Treatment of Schizophrenia: A Comparative*

Study of Five Treatment Methods. New York: Science House, 1968.
21. CARPENTER, W. T., JR., MCGLASHAN, T. H., and STRAUSS, J. S.: Psychosocial treatment of acute schizophrenia. Presented at Annual Meeting of the American Psychiatric Association, Anaheim, California, May 1975.
22. FEINSILVER, D. B. and GUNDERSON, J. G.: Psychotherapy for schizophrenia—is it indicated? A review of the relevant literature. *Schizophrenia Bull.*, 6:11-23, 1972.
23. STRAUSS, J. S. and CARPENTER, W. T., JR.: The evaluation of outcome in schizophrenia. In D. Ricks, A. Thomas, and M. Roff (Eds.): *Life History Research in Psychopathology*, Vol. 3. Minneapolis, Minn.: University of Minnesota Press, 1974.
24. STRAUSS, J. S. and CARPENTER, W. T., JR.: The prediction of outcome in schizophrenia. I. Characteristics of outcome. *Arch. Gen. Psychiatry*, 27:739-746, 1972.
25. FREUD, S.: *Psychoanalytical Notes on an Autobiographical Account of a Case of Paranoia.* S.E., 12:3-82. London: Hogarth Press, 1958.
26. FREUD, S.: *Further Remarks on the Neuropsychoses of Defense.* S.E., 3:157-185. London: Hogarth Press, 1953.
27. GUNDERSON, J. G.: The current metapsychology of schizophrenia. In J. Gunderson and L. Mosher (Eds.): *The Therapy of Schizophrenia as Practiced, Conceptualized and Researched by Experienced Psychotherapists.* New York: Jason Aronson, Inc., in press.
28. HOLZMAN, P. S.: The influence of theoretical models on the treatment of the schizophrenias. Presented at a Panel Discussion on *The Psychotherapy of Schizophrenia*, American Psychoanalytic Association, Dec. 1, 1972, New York, New York.
29. RADO, S.: Schizotypal organization; Preliminary report on a clinical study of schizophrenia. In *Psychoanalysis of Behavior*, Vol. 2, p. 1. New York: Grune & Stratton, 1956.
30. ROSENFELD, H.: *Psychotic States—A Psychoanalytic Approach.* New York: International Universities Press, 1966.
31. SEGAL, H.: Some aspects of the analysis of a schizophrenic. *Int. J. Psychoanal.*, 31:285, 1951.
32. ARLOW, J. and BRENNER, C.: *Psychoanalytic Concepts and the Structural Theory.* New York: International Universities Press, 1964.
33. FROMM-REICHMAN, F.: *Principles of Intensive Psychotherapy.* Chicago: University of Chicago Press, 1950.
34. GRINKER, R.: Changing styles in psychiatric syndromes. *Am. J. Psychiatry*, 130:146-155, 1973.
35. BURNHAM, D. L., GLADSTONE, A. I., and GIBSON, R. W.: *Schizophrenia and the Need-Fear Dilemma.* New York: International Universities Press, Inc., 1969.
36. ARONSON, G.: Defense and deficit models of schizophrenia. Pre-

sented at the Fall meeting of the American Psychoanalytic Association, 1972.
37. Pao, P.: The relationship of the infantile period to the etiology of schizophrenia. Presented at the Fall meeting of the American Psychoanalytic Association, 1974.
38. Mahler, M. S.: On human symbiosis and the vicissitudes of individuation. In *Infantile Psychosis*. New York: International Universities Press, 1968.
39. Gunderson, J. G.: The influence of theoretical model of schizophrenia on treatment practice (Panel Report). *J. Am. Psychoanal. Assoc.*, 22(1):182-199, 1974.
40. Wexler, M.: Schizophrenia: Conflict and deficiency. *Psychoanal. Q.*, 40:83-99, 1971.
41. Searles, H. F.: Discussion: Panel on the influence of theoretical model of schizophrenia on treatment practice. Presented at the Fall meeting of the American Psychoanalytic Association, 1972.
42. Will, O. A.: The psychotherapeutic center and schizophrenia. In R. Cancro (Ed.): *The Schizophrenic Reactions*. New York: Brunner/Mazel, 1970.
43. Arieti, S.: *Interpretation of Schizophrenia*, 2nd Edition. New York: Basic Books, Inc., 1974.
44. Wynne, L. C. and Singer, M. T.: Thought disorder and family relations of schizophrenics: II. A classification of forms of thinking. *Arch. Gen. Psychiatry*, 9:199-206, 1963a.
45. Wynne, L. C. and Singer, M. T.: Thought disorder and family relations of schizophrenics: I. A research strategy. *Arch. Gen. Psychiatry*, 9:191-198, 1963b.
46. Singer, M. T. and Wynne, L. C.: Thought disorder and family relations of schizophrenics: IV. Results and implications. *Arch. Gen. Psychiatry*, 12:201-212, 1965.
47. Wynne, L. C., Singer, M. T., Bartko, J. J., and Toohey, M. L.: Schizophrenics and their families: Recent research on parental communication. To be published in J. M. Tanner (Ed.): *Psychiatric Research: The Widening Perspective*. International Universities Press, 1975.
48. Lidz, T.: *The Origin and Treatment of Schizophrenic Disorders*. New York: Basic Books, Inc., 1973.
49. Searles, H. F.: *Collected Papers on Schizophrenia and Related Subjects*. New York: International Universities Press, 1965.
50. Lidz, T.: Letter to the Editor. *Am. J. Psychiatry*, 131 (9):1039-1041, Sept. 1974.
51. Escalona, S. K.: Patterns of infantile experience and the developmental process. *Psychoanal. Study Child*, 18:197-246, 1963.
52. Mahler, M. and Gosliner, B. J.: On symbiotic child psychosis. *Psychoanal. Study Child*, 10:195-212, 1955.
53. Bender, L.: Childhood schizophrenia. *Am. J. Orthopsychiatry*, 17:40-56, 1947.

54. LAING, R.: *The Politics of Experience.* New York: Pantheon, 1967.
55. VON DOMARUS, E.: The specific laws of logic in schizophrenia. In J. S. Kasanin (Ed.): *Language and Thought in Schizophrenia.* New York: W. W. Norton and Co., 1964.
56. VIGOTSKY, L. S.: Thought in schizophrenia. *Arch. Neurol. and Psychiat.,* 31:1063-1077, 1934.
57. BATESON, G., JACKSON, D. D., HALEY, J., and WEAKLAND, J. H.: Toward a theory of schizophrenia. *Behav. Sci.,* 1:251-264, 1956.
58. WEAKLAND, J. H.: The double-bind hypothesis of schizophrenia and three-party interaction. In D. D. Jackson (Ed.): *The Etiology of Schizophrenia.* New York: Basic Books, Inc., 1960, pp. 373-388.
59. WYNNE, L. C., RYCKOFF, I., DAY, J., and HIRSCH, S.: Pseudomutuality in the family relations of schizophrenics. *Psychiatry,* 21:205-220, 1958.
60. SLUZKI, C. E. and VERON, E.: The double-bind as a universal pathogenic situation. *Fam. Proc.,* 10:397-410, 1971.
61. STIERLIN, H.: *Separating Parents and Adolescents: A Perspective on Schizophrenia, Runaways, and Waywardness.* New York: Quadrangle, 1974.
62. Personal communication by Lidz, ref. 48, above, pp. 66.
63. REISS, D.: Varieties of consensual experience: III. Contrasts between families of normals, delinquents and schizophrenics. *J. Nerv. Ment. Dis.,* 152:73-95, 1971.
64. MISHLER, E. G. and WAXLER, N. E.: *Interaction in Families. An Experimental Study of Family Processes and Schizophrenia.* New York: Wiley, 1968.
65. REISS, D. and WYATT, R. J.: Family and biologic variables in the same etiologic studies of schizophrenia. To be published in *Schizophrenia Bulletin.*
66. ALTSCHULE, M. D.: Disease entity, syndrome, state of mind, or figment? In R. Cancro (Ed.): *The Schizophrenic Reactions.* New York: Brunner/Mazel, 1970.
67. CANCRO, R.: Quoted in *Clinical Psychiatric News,* 7:1, 1974.
68. MOSHER, L. R. and GUNDERSON, J. G.: Special report on schizophrenia: 1972. *Schizophrenia Bulletin,* No. 7, Winter, 1973, pp. 10-52.

5

The Clinical Relevance of Recent Research for Treatment and Prevention of Schizophrenia

Gerald L. Klerman, M.D.

I. Introduction

We are in a period of considerable excitement and progress in research on schizophrenia, particularly its biological aspects. In large part, this research has been stimulated by the therapeutic successes of the phenothiazines and other anti-psychotic agents. The research on neuropharmacology has developed rapidly and has been joined by imaginative studies on genetics, developmental psychology, neurophysiology, and neurochemistry of schizophrenia.

Biological research recently has, in large part, overshadowed much of the research effort in psychodynamics, social psychiatry, and epidemiology. Extending the definition of biology to include aspects of epidemiology and ecology has helped to bring the findings of biological laboratory sciences into clinical relevance.

Supported in part by Research Grant MH24976 from NIMH, ADAMNA, PHS, HEW, Rockville, Maryland.

This research has considerable relevance, and its findings and trends are best understood within the tradition of modern medical research which builds upon the twin concepts of disease and the medical model. It is fashionable in many circles, both within psychiatry and in the larger society, to criticize the medical model. In some circles, the medical model has even become a term of disapprobation. Nevertheless, I want to bring the chronic disease approach to bear upon certain research findings. I shall attempt to explicate the historical and conceptual basis of this approach and demonstrate how the medical model, when applied to schizophrenia, produces the most useful means of (1) integrating the available knowledge, (2) relating it to clinical practice, and (3) developing a public health approach to community mental health and to national policy. The chronic disease approach of the medical model involves a hypothesis, and, like other scientific efforts, it must be validated. There are alternative—and often competing—approaches, such as that of social deviance or the approach of psychodynamic theory, which also involve hypotheses. Ultimately, the question will have to be raised as to what data would be most likely to verify the competing approaches.

I shall touch upon these issues by describing my understanding of the disease approach in medicine at large and in psychiatry by applying it to schizophrenia. Having done so, I will apply it to the needs of the clinician responsible for the care, management, and treatment of the individual schizophrenic patient, and to the administrator responsible for a psychiatric hospital or community mental health program. In conclusion, I will make some general comments about the implications of such an approach for national policy in mental health.

II. The Chronic Disease Approach Applied to Schizophrenia

The first premise of the disease approach is that a group of behaviors such as those now called schizophrenia are psychopathological. I, among others, have concluded from the research evidence and my clinical experience that the experiences of individuals labeled schizophrenic are abnormal. They are distressing to the individual and to those around him. These experiences are profoundly maladaptive for the individual in relationship to his family and his social groupings. While there may be similarities and continuities between the schizophrenic's experience and the emotional life of "normals," yet the schizophrenic state, by virtue of its intensity, persistence, and degree of interference with the usual psychological, cognitive, and perceptual norms and with accepted social behavior, is best regarded as one of illness, and the disease concept is the most applicable.

In taking this position I am firmly opposed to the view of Szasz that mental illness in general, and schizophrenia in particular, is a myth. If it is a myth, then the individuals who are schizophrenic are doubly delusional in their suffering. It would also have to be a myth with a genetic basis, as Kety has said, and with a pharmacological antidote (1975). My position is also opposed to that of Laing and many of the family therapists who deny that there is such a thing as a patient per se and who state that the locus of pathology is in the family or in the society at large. While there are important familial and social influences upon the epidemiology of schizophrenia and the life of the individual schizophrenic, it is an odd form of sophistry to deny the sick role and the advantages of being treated to the patient while displacing responsibility (or is it blame?) to the family at large. In this aspect I am in agreement with Siegler and Osmond in their recent book, *Models of Madness* (1974). I am strongly disagreeing with the labeling school of sociology and social psychology, particularly Scheff (1964) and Rosenhan (1973), who say that the problems of the schizophrenic are mainly due to the way in which we psychiatrists label him and the society rejects him. Such processes may indeed go on, but they do not obviate the primary inherent difficulties that the schizophrenic experiences in his attempts at life adjustment.

As the concept of disease is not a given, it must be achieved as a result of the accumulation of research. The criteria for such a disease concept developed within the traditional model in the seventeenth century through the observations of Sydenham and others, who conceived of disease states as having qualities of their own with characteristic symptoms and natural history. For general medicine the disease concept was crystallized in the mid-nineteenth century by Virchow who united Sydenham's observation of clinical patterns with the findings of pathological anatomy from the autopsy room and with the bacteriological findings of Pasteur and others. It was not until the late nineteenth century that this concept of disease entities related to etiology was applied to mental disorders by the generation of Kraepelin (1921) and Bleuler (1951). At that time, the main clinical problem was the development of criteria for separating the larger group of psychotic conditions into those with some established origin. Kraepelin's main achievement was twofold. First, he was the most persistent in applying the etiological approach to disease to mental disorders, in contrast to the predominantly symptomatic approaches which prevailed during the earlier part of the nineteenth century. Applying etiological principles, he was able to classify disordered states on the basis of their being infectious, toxic, traumatic, etc., leaving a residual category of functional psychoses with no apparent etiology. He then subdivided this group of functional psychoses into dementia praecox and manic-depressive insanity.

Thus Kraepelin's second major achievement was the delineation to two types of psychoses from among those of the group without any apparent etiology.

Bleuler later renamed dementia praecox *schizophrenia* because of his observation that the cognitive disturbance was not that of dementia but that of an associational defect. Over the succeeding three-quarters of the century, psychiatry has extended its boundaries beyond the mental hospital and psychopathology and has been concerned with conditions other than psychoses. Nevertheless, recent research, particularly since World War II, has established the validity of the distinction between these two major psychotic states. Although the medical model and descriptive approaches ran into some disrepute with the dominance of the psychoanalytic school in American psychiatry after World War II, recent research has vindicated the basic strength of the medical model, particularly when applied to schizophrenia.

How well then does schizophrenia meet the criteria of a chronic disease in the medical model? I conclude that it meets it well but not completely. Before one can conclude definitely that schizophrenia is a disease, further data will have to be presented as to its etiology and clinical course. While a good bit of such data exist for many other disorders in psychiatry, this is not the case in schizophrenia. Schizophrenia, thus, is like many of the other clinical conditions with which medicine deals, such as hypertension, arthritis, and leukemia. That is to say, it is an obviously disordered state with multiple determinants in which there is not certainty as to the exact etiology. Moreover, it is similar to hypertension in that it is likely that schizophrenia, as we now define it, is comprised of various disorders. As the specific etiological principles come under scientific investigation, we will reaffirm Bleuler's concept of a group of schizophrenias. Nevertheless, it is likely that within this group of schizophrenias there is a core group which has a strong genetic component as validated by such twin studies and adoption studies as those of Kety and his associates (1968). The genetic basis provides for a vulnerability which becomes manifest in psychoses when precipitated by environmental stresses.

I have mentioned that schizophrenia is best approached from a chronic disease approach. The chronic disease approach is a sub-variant of the disease approach. The classic disease approach deals with acute states such as those brought on by trauma and infection, and deals with illness of relatively short duration. In contrast, the chronic disease approach contains a number of common features, such as mixed source of etiology, no cure, and long course with intermittent recurrences. The goal in the chronic disease approach is prevention of disability and complications. Most conditions with which medicine deals today are chronic conditions.

Some chronic diseases have established etiologies, as in the case of tuberculosis or syphilis. Syphilitic illness of the brain is one classic example of chronic psychiatric illness with a known etiology which responded to research in the medical model. When we come to schizophrenia we are faced with a problem similar to those faced by our colleagues in internal medicine who treat hypertension, arthritis, or leukemia, in that the etiology of these diseases is not known and there may be more than one etiological disease entity presenting with a common clinical syndrome.

Similarly to hypertension, arthritis, and leukemia, schizophrenia represents a symptom complex whose boundaries are at times not clearly demarcated but have a certain degree of unity in clinical presentation and characteristic course of the group as a whole. Nevertheless, within the group there is considerable variation among individuals. Moreover, there is uncertainty as to whether the group represents a single etiological entity or, as is most likely the case, a complex of multiple entities.

The best example in psychiatry of such a grouping is mental retardation. With the success of biological investigation of the aminoacidurias and chromosomal abnormalities, the large heterogeneous grouping of mental deficiency is being broken down. Such a process will soon be underway in schizophrenia. In fact, it is foreshadowed in the delineation of those schizophrenic syndromes due to drugs (such as amphetamines) as distinguished from those associated with epilepsy or diseases such as lupus.

III. Clinical Treatment

For the clinician responsible for the care, treatment, and management of individual patients, recent decades have seen an explosion of research which is highly relevant to his practice. The clinician is interested in a number of topics: diagnosis, treatment, use of drugs for the acute episode, the role of hospitalization, maintenance drug treatment, the role of the family, and the role of psychotherapy. Let me take up each of these topics in order.

(1) *Diagnosis*

It must be acknowledged that there has been considerable erosion in the previous precision (or pseudoprecision) with which descriptive psychopathologic terms have been used. There has been some excellent recent research on diagnostic practice, notably by Katz and Cole (1969), Spitzer (1968), and Robins (1970) in the U.S., by Wing (1967) and Kendell (1968) in England, and by the WHO group (Sartorius, 1974). The evidence from these researchers indicates that there has been an unnecessarily wide divergence in the criteria for the definition of schizophrenia. The criteria for making the diagnosis are rarely stipulated in the clinical discussions or in the research literature. As Sharpe (1974) points out, considerable differences exist among psychiatrists in various countries in the use of diagnostic labels. These differences are particularly pronounced between American psychiatrists and our colleagues in Britain and Europe. The work of the US-UK project demonstrates that psychiatrists in New York diagnose schizophrenia in a group of patients whom British and Continental European psychiatrists call schizophrenic, but in addition American psychiatrists include patients with mania, psychotic depression, and personality disorder in the schizophrenic category. This American tendency to expand the boundaries of schizophrenia to make it almost all-inclusive of psychoses and, at times, of all severe psychiatric disturbances, not only creates difficulty in comparison between our experiences and those of our colleagues in Britain and the Continent, but favors a breakdown in the practice of differential diagnosis.

Differential diagnosis is important for two reasons. First, there are a number of defined syndromes which may present with a schizophrenic-like picture. These include some medical conditions, such as lupus, and neurological diseases, such as temporal lobe epilepsy. They also include common drug syndromes, particularly in young people, such as amphetamine abuse and that of LSD and related psychotomimetic drugs. Second, with the availability of effective treatments for psychotic depression and mania, careful attention to the syndromal diagnoses is important.

(2) *Treatment of the Acute Episode*

Assuming that the diagnostic process has been thorough and that a differential diagnosis has been undertaken, the treatment of the acute episode can be highly gratifying. Phenothiazine treatment or treatment with other antipsychotic (neuroleptic) drugs is the mainstay of the treatment of acute psychotic episodes of a schizophrenic nature. Extensive research on clinical trials by the VA (Caffey, 1967), NIMH (1964), and other groups has indicated the essential unity of clinical response to four or five classes of antipsychotic drugs. Attempts to find specific criteria and symptoms or backgrounds for selecting one antipsychotic drug over another have not proven to be replicable.

The question arises as to the possible value of psychotherapy for the acute episode. There is no controlled study which indicates any value for psychotherapy as a *specific* treatment. Rather the emphasis should be placed on what May has called "psychotherapeutic management," that is, attention to the individual needs of the patient, maintenance of open communication, furthering of empathy and understanding, and laying the groundwork for long-term treatment.

(3) *Lessons from Pharmacotherapy*

Treatments used in chronic disease usually make the patient better but not completely well. It is fashionable in many circles to depreciate the available drugs as only being symptomatic or palliative. The conventional wisdom juxtaposes fully curative agents such as antibiotics with symptomatic agents. However, this is unfair. There should be a middle ground of agents such as the phenothiazines, the tricyclic antidepressants, the diuretic antihypertensives, and the anticonvulsants. These drugs, which do more than offer purely symptomatic relief, interfere with the symptom formation in such a way as to facilitate the patient's recompensation and make him better although they do not remove any etiological process.

In fact, this is probably one of the lessons from the neuropharmacology of the antipsychotic drugs. The unity of action both clinically and neuropharmacologically in the phenothiazines, the butyrophenones, and the other classes of the antipsychotic drugs is strong suggestion of a common core of altered neurochemical metabolism, probably involving dopamine, reflected in a common pattern of symptom presentation and a common pattern of response to available treatments. These factors together reinforce the utility and validity of the concept of schizophrenia. Whatever further classification is arrived at, there does seem to be some common pathway of symptom formation which is interrupted by the available drugs in a manner similar to the way in which the diuretics interrupt the mechanisms responsible for elevated blood pressure, whether this is due to essential hypertension or kidney disease.

(4) *Role of Hospitalization*

The role of the hospital, at least during the acute episode, seems to be that of crisis intervention and helping the patient over the psychotic stage. In this sense, hospitalization plays the same role for the schizophrenic as it does for the arthritic, cardiac, or hepatic patient. In the past, some psychotherapeutically oriented hospitals set as their goal the restructuring of the underlying personality of the individual, the attempt to undo presumed pathogenic influences of family patterns in early childhood or on the ongoing communication pattern. There is no research evidence that this is effective. In fact, most of the evidence indicates that the adverse effects of dependency and institutionalism far outweigh any advantage of long-term hospitalization. We still do not have good data as to the optimum length of hospitalization for the acute episode. Although the national average indicates about 20-30 days for psychiatric hospitalization in general hospital units, there is some evidence that schizophrenic episodes might do better with a more prolonged period. However, more definitive research is desirable.

Recent epidemiologic research indicates an important shift in the locus of hospital treatment. Whereas in the past 80% of all inpatient care was given in public mental hospitals, mostly VA and state mental hospitals, today 40-50% of all inpatient episodes take place in psychiatric units of general hospitals (Kramer, 1969). This trend is increasing rapidly with the greater public acceptance of such units and with third party reimbursement. There are many advantages to treating acute schizophrenic episodes in a general hospital. One of these is the opportunity for a careful differential diagnosis of neurological, medical, and toxicologic conditions. The other is the availability of carefully trained personnel for the monitoring of intensive drug management.

Although considerable research has been done on extra-hospital treatment of the acute episode, the hospital still remains the main locus for the treatment of the acute schizophrenic psychotic episode. Research such as that done by Pasamanick (1967) indicates that home treatment with visiting nurse personnel is often highly effective. Similarly, studies on day treatment centers indicate their efficacy. One is hard-pressed to understand why these carefully controlled trials have not been generally accepted into clinical practice. Perhaps it is because of the inherent conservatism of the reimbursement process whereby insurance companies have not seen fit to reimburse treatment in home visits or day treatment.

(5) *Maintenance Drug Therapy*

Once the patient has resolved the acute psychotic episode, transfer from the hospital setting to a community setting is common, feasible, and effective. The most difficult problem has to do with the planning for treatment of patients who have had their first psychotic episode. Inasmuch as there is uncertainty as to the boundaries of psychosis, we must acknowledge that not all patients who have acute psychotic episodes, particularly with onset in young adulthood, are necessarily schizophrenic. We must be prepared to accept the concept of psychosis of undetermined etiology, comprising conditions variously called schizo-affective, reactive psychosis, schizophreniform psychosis, and borderline states. Therefore, it would be an error to place all patients who experience a psychotic episode on phenothiazine maintenance. Particularly after the first episode a period of tapering off and gradual reduction of the dosage over three to six months would seem useful. Although excellent work has been done on predictors of response to treatment, we still do not have sufficiently clear guides as to how best to manage the patients recovering from the first episode. It may well be that these patients would benefit from individual and/or group psychotherapy.

With regard to planning for long-term maintenance therapy, alternative approaches have been used. Some therapists give blanket maintenance therapy to all individuals who have had psychotic episodes in an attempt to cover that proportion of the population who are likely to benefit. Others attempt to restrict maintenance therapy to only those patients with two or more episodes for whom withdrawal and discontinuation of drug therapy have failed. Aside from financial reasons, there is an important consideration which merits selection of the second strategy—the development of side effects.

(6) *Tardive Dyskinesia*

We now know that there are definite hazards associated with long-term antipsychotic drug treatment, mainly that of tardive dyskinesia. Often irreversible and incapacitating, these dyskinesias tend to develop in female patients, over fifty years old, with a history of family involvement in neurological disease, who have been on the drug for a long period of time. There seems to be a relationship between cumulative dosage of antipsychotic drugs and susceptibility to irreversible dyskinesia. Use of anti-Parkinsonian drugs over a long period of time does not seem to prevent the development of incapacitation from dyskinesia. Given this difficulty, there are important reasons to select carefully the patients who require long-term treatment.

(7) *The Role of the Family*

While the initial hope for family therapy as curative in schizophrenia has not been realized, more conservative approaches to understanding family dynamics have generated important findings, such as the earlier work of Freeman and Simmons which indicated that patients returning to situations of high expectations tended to be under considerable stress. This work has been extended by the research of Leff and Wing (1971), Brown (1972), and Hirsch (1972). Their work indicates that schizophrenics in the community do poorly in settings which are very socially deprived, such as the back wards of state hospitals, or at the other extreme where there is intense social stimulation and the overt expression of emotion, particularly hostility and fear. There seems to be a middle ground wherein the patient is not over-stimulated by too much social interaction and affective expression and yet not under-stimulated and allowed to withdraw. There is a relationship, as yet unspecified, between this optimal level of stimulation and the availability of a family. Schizophrenics who never marry or who are without any parental or familial relations have a very poor prognosis. Studies by Kramer and others of patients with long-term residence in state hospitals indicate that the majority of these patients have no social family supports, poor education, and lower socio-economic background.

These family factors are related to the role of pre-morbid social competence as has been shown by Vaillant (1964), Garmezy (in press), Rodnick (1973), and others who have been involved in various prognostic studies. In general, the better the patient premorbidly, particularly in adolescent socialization, occupational adjustment, and level of achievement, the better the prognosis not only for recovery of the acute episode but for re-entry into, and maintenance of social function in, the community.

(8) *The Role of Psychotherapy*

Supportive psychotherapy geared towards helping the patient readapt to community roles has definitely been established as having an important place. This can be done either by group or individual social work contact or by individual or group contact with the psychiatrist. Studies by Hogarty and Goldberg (1973) in Baltimore indicate that social therapies, particularly those geared towards the "here and now," are most effective in the presence of antipsychotic maintenance therapy. Without such drug therapy, particularly with chronic patients, psychotherapy alone has little efficacy.

(9) *Summary*

If the clinician adopts the view that schizophrenia is a chronic illness, he will see his role as that of offering care, maintenance, and treatment aimed at maximizing the patient's inherent resources. He will proceed towards this goal by using available drug treatments to minimize symptomatology and by making use of family, community and other resources to facilitate the patient's rehabilitation. Thus the clinician concerned with the treatment of schizophrenia is inevitably drawn to involvement with community planning for treatment facilities and the preventative approach.

IV. Prevention: Implications for Community Mental Health

Psychiatrists who are responsible for programs at an institutional or community mental health level are concerned not only with the treatment of individual patients but also about developing a network of services and programs which can maximize the availability of treatment to all the schizophrenics in the community, lower costs, increase efficiency, and, hopefully, develop prevention.

In talking about prevention, I have found it useful to apply the concepts developed in public health that distinguish between primary, secondary, and tertiary prevention.

(1) *Primary prevention* refers to attempts to affect etiologic changes before the onset of manifest symptoms. The classic example of success in primary prevention is immunization for smallpox, diphtheria, or polio, or chlorination of water.

(2) *Secondary prevention* refers to early identification of cases and maximum application of available techniques to reduce mortality, reduce duration of illness, and minimize residual disability. Most clinical medicine, as we know it, falls into the category of secondary prevention.

(3) *Tertiary prevention,* or rehabilitation, aims at meeting the needs of patients with chronic illnesses or the residual acute illnesses in order to maximize their social, occupational, and personal adjustment.

(1) *Primary Prevention*

As regards primary prevention, we must concede only a minimal knowledge and available technique. The genetic studies would seem to suggest the possible value of genetic counseling although the basis for this is still primitive in the field of schizophrenia. Another aspect of primary prevention is the selection of high risk populations, such as the children or siblings of schizophrenics, and early intervention in the preschool or adolescent period of these high risk groups. The problem here is the lack of criteria for identifying high risk groups and, while this research is now underway in the work of Garmezy, Wynne and Romano in Rochester, and Mednick in Scandinavia, we are not yet assured of any results which have practical advantages for immediate application, although there is promise in this area for the future (Garmezy, 1974).

Another aspect of primary prevention would be that of contraception and family planning. Whether one accepts a genetic mode of transmission or that of familial influence, schizophrenics make poor parents, and the offspring of families in which one or both parents are schizophrenic are very much at risk for subsequent illness. More attention to family planning and use of contraception would, therefore, clearly seem to have a potential for primary prevention.

Efforts at primary prevention through community organization, consultation with schools, or family education would seem to offer only minimum hope of achievement considering the relatively low incidence of schizophrenia in the population as a whole and our lack of knowledge as to the precise roles of various familial and social influences. Poverty and overall social conditions have been implicated in epidemiologic studies such as that of Hollingshead and Redlich (1958) in New Haven and Srole et al. (1961) in midtown Manhattan. The implications of this for primary prevention other than the general improvement of the welfare and economic well-being of the population at large are unclear.

(2) *Secondary Prevention*

Secondary prevention involves early case findings and intensive treatment to minimize disability. In this area we have made substantial progress. The main thrust of the community mental health movement has been highly successful in maximizing the availability of treatment resources to many populations for whom such treatment was previously inaccessible either because of geography along racial and ethnic barriers or financial cost. The evidence indicates that recent years have seen a great social leveling as regards the availability of treatment for schizophrenics and an improvement in the quality of treatment for the acute episode so that the duration of disability and symptomatology is much decreased. Mortality, which was considerable before World Wars I and II, has been reduced to almost zero. The duration of symptomatology is much reduced, and the probability of remission and return to the community is very high. Over 70-80% of patients with acute psychotic schizophrenic episodes can look forward to remission of the acute episode and return to the community.

(3) *Tertiary Prevention-Rehabilitation*

Tertiary prevention refers to rehabilitation. The gap between research knowledge and actual practice is appallingly great. Ample research had been done in the 1950's and early 1960's identifying those conditions which facilitate the rehabilitation of the schizophrenic either in an institution or in the community. Parallel research had identified sources of stress and adverse features which would maximize the conditions under which schizophrenics would do poorly. The early hope of the community mental health movement was that this knowledge would be applied simultaneously to phase out the large state hospitals and to create an adequate network of community resources.

Research recently undertaken to determine the quality of life of schizophrenics still residing in public mental hospitals indicates that there are appalling conditions of continued institutionalism, dehumanization, and deindividualization. Whatever the criticisms which apply to conclusions in Rosenhan's study pertaining to diagnosis and the medical model (Spitzer, in press), we cannot ignore the findings documenting the impersonality of mental hospitals and the staff's tendency to disregard the individual needs of patients. Although the census of state mental hospitals has decreased greatly, the quality of treatment has not significantly improved. The available studies as to these issues indicate that patients residing in public mental hospitals are still subject to poor treatment and tend towards the phenomenon of institutionalization identified by Goffman and other sociologists in the 1950's.

The situation is little better for those patients in the community. New forms of community chronicity have been developed in many large urban settings such as New York, Chicago,

Los Angeles, and San Francisco. In the absence of an adequate network of after-care facilities, community residences and halfway houses, sheltered workshops, and day treatment centers, large numbers of patients are relegated to "lives of quiet desperation" in welfare hotels and segregated neighborhoods, are subsisting on minimal incomes from social welfare or disability payments, and are receiving poorly monitored, often poorly prescribed, psychotropic medication. When one compares this picture of a large number of schizophrenic patients with the potential that had been demonstrated in the imaginative research programs in the 1950's and 1960's, one is appalled and dismayed. Research studies such as those by Gruenberg (1962), by Fairweather (1969), by the Fountain House group in New York, and others indicated that the combination of antipsychotic drug medication plus the availability of a network of rehabilitative, vocational, and properly supervised residential facilities could reduce the disability and social isolation of schizophrenics.

It is not possible for me to discern what went wrong. The promise of the community mental health program has only been partially realized. Application of the available knowledge failed to materialize except in a few selected community mental health centers. Perhaps the mental health movement grew overambitious and too quickly expanded its responsibility in the late 1960's into alcoholism, drug abuse, racism, and social unrest, without being sure that the problems of the schizophrenics, one of our primary clinical obligations, had been met. Perhaps it has been a failure of the National Institute of Mental Health to assign priority and resources to this need. Perhaps it has been an overestimate of the extent to which community attitudes had, in fact, changed. Whatever the reasons, the community treatment of schizophrenia remains an area of high relevance but low success (Klerman, 1974).

V. Conclusions: Implications for the Profession and for National Policy

The research underway, mainly in the biological sciences and also in the related fields of social psychiatry, epidemiology, and psychology, is most directly relevant to the clinician responsible for the care of individual patients. It is also, as I have hoped to indicate, applicable to the mental health administrator responsible for developing programs of a preventive nature using a public health model. But what of our national policy? This is a time of considerable unrest within the profession and of criticism of psychiatry from without. This criticism is often reflected in decisions of legislators and budget bureaus at the municipal, county, and state level.

My conclusion is obvious. Psychiatry is part of the practice of medicine. The public expects mental illness to be treated within a medical healing model. The public expects psychiatrists to behave as physicians. The public and community leaders are willing to see us expand our horizons to include psychotherapeutic and social psychiatric approaches as part of a comprehensive program, but not in place of a medical approach. When we stray from the medical model, particularly as regards schizophrenia, we are in serious jeopardy, and this may well have been the case in respect to the events of the late 1960's and early 1970's. In this respect the biological researchers who reported in this symposium have helped keep us honest. The quality of their research in genetics, neurophysiology, neurochemistry, and pharmacology is impressive.

There seems, however, to be a clear split within the profession. Within the research community the biological tradition has gained great strength and esteem and the disease model has achieved considerable resurgence of respectability. Within the profession as a whole, the trends are less clear. Many of us as psychiatrists remain ambivalent about our medical identity.

We are the only professional group legally empowered and professionally trained to use drugs, and yet, in practice, many, if not most, psychiatrists do so with reluctance, ambivalence, hesitation, and ignorance of findings from basic biological science. We, as a profession, have extended our scope into problems of neuroses, personality development, social change, and this is fine, although in these other fields we share a responsibility with education, clinical psychology, and social work. We cannot forget, however, that we, among all the professions, have accepted the responsibility for the psychoses.

The most influential leadership is that of Washington, and it is important that our colleagues at the National Institute of Mental Health see these trends for their political and policy implications. In developing a research and training program, leadership in the executive and legislative branches should pay heed to the relevance of the medical model and the strength of biological research. Any national program that attempts to ignore psychopharmacology or biological research does so at its own jeopardy. Any national policy which supports, directly or indirectly, the deprecation and denunciation of the medical model flies in the face of established scientific evidence which I hope I have shown to be relevant to the clinician, the administrator, and the policy maker.

REFERENCES

BLEULER, E.: *Textbook of Psychiatry*. An Authorized English Edition. Brill, E. (Ed.). New York: Dover Publications, 1951.
BROWN, G. W., BIRLEY, J. L. T. and WING, J. K.: Influence of family life on the course of schizophrenic disorders: A replication. *Brit. J. Psych.*, 121:241-258, 1972.
CAFFEY, J. R., JONES, R. D., BURTON, E., DIAMOND, L. S., and BOWEN, W. T.: A controlled study of brief hospitalization for schizophrenics, Veterans Administration, Cooperative Studies in Psychiatry, Central Neuropsychiatric Research Laboratory, Perry Point, Maryland, 1967.
FAIRWEATHER, G. W., SANDERS, D. H., CRESSLER, D. L., and MAYNARD,

H.: *Community Life for the Mentally Ill.* Chicago: Aldine Publishing Co., 1969.

GARMEZY, N.: Children at risk: The search for the antecedents of schizophrenia. Part II: Ongoing research programs, issues, and intervention. *Schizophrenia Bulletin.* NIMH, Center for the Study of Schizophrenia, 9:55-125, 1974.

GARMEZY, N.: The study of competence in children at risk for severe psychopathology. In: *Children at Psychiatric Risk.* E. Anthony and C. Koupernik (Eds.). New York: John Wiley and Sons (in press).

GRUENBERG, E. M., KASIUS, R. V., and HUXLEY, M.: Objective appraisal of deterioration in a group of long-stay hospital patients. *Millbank Memorial Fund Quarterly,* 60:1-11, 1962.

HIRSCH, S. R., GAIND, R., and ROHDE, P.: The clinical value of Fluphenazine Deconante in maintaining chronic schizophrenics in the community. Presented at the International Symposium on Rehabilitation in Psychiatry, Belgrade, Yugoslavia, June 21-24, 1972.

HOLLINGSHEAD, A. B. and REDLICH, F. C.: *Social Class and Mental Illness.* New York: John Wiley and Sons, Inc., 1958.

HOGARTY, G. E. and GOLDBERG, S. C.: Drugs and sociotherapy in the after-care of schizophrenic patients. *Arch. Gen. Psych.,* 28:54-62, 1973.

KATZ, M. M., COLE, J. O., and LOWERY, H. A.: Studies of the diagnostic process: The influence of symptom perception, past experience, and ethnic background on diagnostic decision. *Am. J. Psych.,* 125:937, 1969.

KENDELL, R. E.: *The Classification of Depressive Illness.* London: Oxford University Press, 1968.

KETY, S. S., ROSENTHAL, D., SCHULSINGER, F., and WENDER, P. H.: The types and prevalence of mental illness in the biological and adoptive families of adopted schizophrenics. *J. Psych. Res.,* 1(Suppl.): 345-362, 1968.

KETY, S.: From rationalization to reason. *Am. J. Psych.,* 131:957-963, 1974.

KLERMAN, G. L.: Current evaluation research on mental health services. *Am. J. Psych.,* 131:783-787, 1974.

KLERMAN, G. L.: Neuroleptics: Too many or too few? Presented at Symposium on Rational Psychopharmacotherapy and the Right to Treatment at Taylor Manor Hospital, Ellicott City, Maryland, October 11-12, 1974.

KRAEPELIN, E.: *Manic Depressive Insanity and Paranoia.* Transl. by M. Barclay. Edinburgh: Livingstone, 1921.

KRAMER, M.: Applications of mental health statistics: Uses in mental health programs of statistics derived from psychiatric services and selected vital and morbidity records. Geneva, Switzerland: World Health Organization, 1969.

LEFF, J. P. and WING, J. K.: Trial of maintenance therapy in schizophrenics. *Brit. Med. J.*, 2:599-604, 1971.
NIMH-PSC Collaborative Study Group: Phenothiazine treatment in acute schizophrenia. *Arch. Gen. Psych.*, 10:246-261, 1964.
PASAMANICK, B., SCARPITTI, F. R., and DINITZ, S.: *Schizophrenics in the Community: An Experimental Study in the Prevention of Hospitalization.* New York: Appleton-Century-Crofts, 1967.
ROBINS, E. and GUZE, S. B.: Establishment of diagnostic validity in psychiatric illness. Its application to schizophrenia. *Am. J. Psych.*, 126:983-988, 1970.
RODNICK, E. H.: Antecedents and continuities in schizophreniform behavior. In: *Schizophrenia: The First Ten Dean Award Lectures.* Dean, S. R. (Ed.), New York: MSS Information Corp., 1973.
ROSENHAN, D. L.: On being in insane places. *Science*, 179:250-258, 1973.
SARTORIUS, N. (Ed.): International Pilot Study of Schizophrenia. World Health Organization Monograph (MH 09239), Geneva, Switzerland, 1974.
SCHEFF, T.: Societal reaction to deviance: Ascriptive elements in the psychiatric screening of mental patients in a midwestern state. *Social Problems*, 11:401-413, 1964.
SHARPE, L., GURLAND, B. J., FLEISS, J. L., KENDELL, R. E., COOPER, J. E., and COPELAND, J. R. M.: Comparisons of American, Canadian and British Psychiatrists in their diagnostic concepts. *Can. Psychiat. Assoc. J.*, 19:235-245, 1974.
SIEGLER, M. and OSMOND, H.: *Models of Madness, Models of Medicine.* New York: Macmillan Publishing Co., 1974.
SPITZER, R. L.: Critique of Rosenhan. *J. Abnormal Psychology* (in press, 1975).
SPITZER, R. L. and WILSON, P. T.: A guide to the American Psychiatric Association's new diagnostic nomenclature. *Am. J. Psych.*, 124:1619-1629, 1968.
SROLE, L., LANGER, T. S., MICHAEL, S. T., OPLER, M. K., and RENNIE, T. A. C.: *Mental Health in the Metropolis.* New York: McGraw-Hill, 1961.
VAILLANT, G.: Prospective prediction of schizophrenic remission. *Arch. Gen. Psych.*, 11:509-518, 1964.
WING, J. K., BIRLEY, J. L. T., COOPER, J. E., GRAHAM, P., and ISAACS, A. D.: Reliability of a procedure for measuring and classifying present psychiatric state. *Brit. J. Psych.*, 113:499-515, 1967.

6

Stanley R. Dean Award Lecture

Pharmacological Approach to Schizophrenia

Arvid Carlsson, M.D., Ph.D.

INTRODUCTION

Schizophrenic symptomatology can be profoundly influenced by drugs: while certain drugs alleviate, others produce or aggravate schizophrenic symptoms. Studies on the mode and site of action of such drugs may yield important clues. The potentiality of this type of approach has been demonstrated, e.g., in the case of Parkinson's disease (1).

I hope you will bear with me if I describe the development in this area more or less in chronological order as I have witnessed it myself.

My active research interest in the antipsychotic agents began just 20 years ago. In 1955-1956, I had the privilege of working in the famous Laboratory of Chemical Pharmacology, headed by Dr. B. B. Brodie, at the National Institutes of Health in Bethesda, Md. This was only a few years after the discovery of the remarkable therapeutic effect of chlorpromazine and reserpine in psychotic conditions such as schizophrenia. Shortly before my arrival Drs. Brodie and Shore had made an important discovery, namely that reserpine is capable of releasing serotonin from its various stores in the body and causing depletion of these stores (2). They speculated that the antipsychotic action of reserpine was due to continuous release of serotonin onto receptors.

I am greatly indebted to Drs. Brodie and Shore for introducing me to this fascinating field of research. After returning to Sweden I found, together with the late Dr. N. -A. Hillarp, that the catecholamines are also released by reserpine (3). This resulted in depletion of the adrenergic transmitter noradrenaline and in failure of adrenergic transmission (4).

Reserpine, Dopa and Dopamine

We felt that deficiency of amines at receptor sites was the most likely explanation of the pharmacological actions of reserpine. To test this hypothesis we gave the catecholamine precursor dopa to reserpine-treated animals and discovered the central activity of this amino acid, presumably mediated via its decarboxylation products (5). The dramatic reversal of the reserpine syndrome by dopa supported our deficiency theory, and the simultaneously observed inefficiency of 5-hydroxytryptophan directed our attention to the catecholamines.

At this time the primary decarboxylation product of dopa, i.e. dopamine, had not yet been detected with certainty in the brain, owing to lack of a specific and sensitive method for assaying this compound. We developed such a method and found that dopamine is stored by a reserpine-sensitive mechanism in the brain in even greater amounts than noradrenaline, suggesting that it is not just an intermediary in the biosynthesis of noradrenaline and adrenaline (6). In support of this, the distribution of dopamine was found to differ greatly from that of noradrenaline, the largest amounts being found in the basal ganglia rather than the brain stem, where noradrenaline occurs in the highest concentration (7).

Brain Monoamines: Neurohumoral Transmitters

The actions of reserpine and dopa, as well as the regional distribution data, suggested to us that the catecholamines are important agonists in the brain and that they (especially dopamine) are involved in the control of extrapyramidal motor functions as well as in higher integrative functions such as wakefulness (8, 9). However, many investigators expressed doubts at this time (around 1960), especially in the case of dopamine, which was known by pharmacologists only as a poor adrenergic agonist. The skepticism was but partly dissipated by Hornykiewicz's discovery of reduced dopamine levels in the brains of Parkinsonian patients (10), or by the subsequent demonstration of the therapeutic properties of L-dopa (11). Probably more instrumental in this respect was the accumulation of evidence demonstrating the role of the brain monoamines as neurohumoral transmitters. Particularly strong support came from the demonstration, by means of fluorescence histochemistry, of the neuronal localization of the brain monoamines (12) and the subsequent mapping out of the monoamine-carrying neuronal pathways (13-16). Electron-microscopical, biochemical and physiological techniques also contributed to make a strong case for the brain monoamines as neurohumoral transmitters: it was established that the monoamines (dopamine, noradrenaline and 5-hydroxytryptamine) are formed in nerve terminals and stored in synaptic vesicles; they are released by nerve stimulation; after release they cause physiological effects; efficient inactivation mechanisms to terminate the action exist; transmitter turnover is markedly dependent on the nerve impulses (for review, see 17).

Receptor-Blocking Antipsychotic Agents

I should like to come back now to the mode of action of the antipsychotic drugs. In the case of reserpine we were rather satisfied with the evidence. Reserpine appears to act by causing transmission failure in monoaminergic nerves, and this is due to depletion of transmitter, which can no longer be concentrated in the synaptic vesicles (or storage granules) because of blockade of a specific uptake mechanism in these organelles (18). In fact, more recent studies, utilizing the principle of selective protection of individual transmitter stores, have confirmed our original suggestions and clearly demonstrated the dominating role of the catecholamines, notably dopamine, for the characteristic syndrome induced by reserpine, even though 5-HT appears to contribute (19).

We were puzzled, however, by the virtual absence of an effect on monoamine levels exerted by some clinically important groups of antipsychotic agents, i.e., the phenothiazines, the thiaxanthenes, the butyrophenones, etc. As is well known, these drugs are remarkably similar to reserpine with respect to the whole spectrum of psychiatric, extrapyramidal, and endocrinological actions, and yet they must have an entirely different mode of action at the molecular level.

In 1963, Margit Lindqvist and I found that small doses of chlorpromazine and haloperidol specifically stimulated the metabolism of dopamine and noradrenaline in mouse brain, and since this took place without any decrease in catecholamine levels, we inferred that the synthesis of the catecholamines was also stimulated by these agents (20). It was known at this time that the central effects of catecholamines (from administered dopa) could be antagonized by these agents, and thus we proposed the following mechanism to account for the observations made. The antipsychotic phenothiazines and butyrophenones act by blocking central dopamine and noradrenaline receptors.

This blockade activates a negative feedback mechanism which leads to an increased physiological activity of catecholamine neurons, with an increased release, metabolism, and synthesis of the transmitter (Fig. 1).

This concept of receptor-mediated feedback control of neuronal activity has been amply confirmed and extended by numerous investigators (17, 21). Also, in man, antipsychotic agents have been found to stimulate central catecholamine metabolism (22). Moreover, the hypothesis that phenothiazines and butyrophenones act by blocking catecholamine receptors has received support through the work of Greengard and his colleagues (23), who have demonstrated what appears to be dopaminergic receptor responsiveness of a cell-free adenylate cyclase system, obtained from striatal tissue. This system can be activated by dopamine, and the effect is blocked by phenothiazines, butyrophenones, etc.

Central noradrenaline receptors, blocked by antipsychotic agents, appear to be similar to the peripheral α-adrenergic receptors. However, central dopamine receptors are different, since either type of receptor can be selectively activated or blocked (24). A survey of the receptor-blocking properties of antipsychotic drugs indicates that all of them, except for those causing monoamine depletion, possess dopamine receptor-blocking activity. In addition, some of them are capable of blocking central α-adrenergic receptors, but certain agents appear to be devoid of such activity while maintaining antipsychotic properties (25, 26). Besides, no antipsychotic action of pure α-adrenergic blocking agents has thus far been reported. From these data the conclusion seems justified that dopamine receptor-blocking activity is essential for the antipsychotic effect. This does not, however, exclude the possibility that noradrenaline-receptor blockade may play a contributory role.

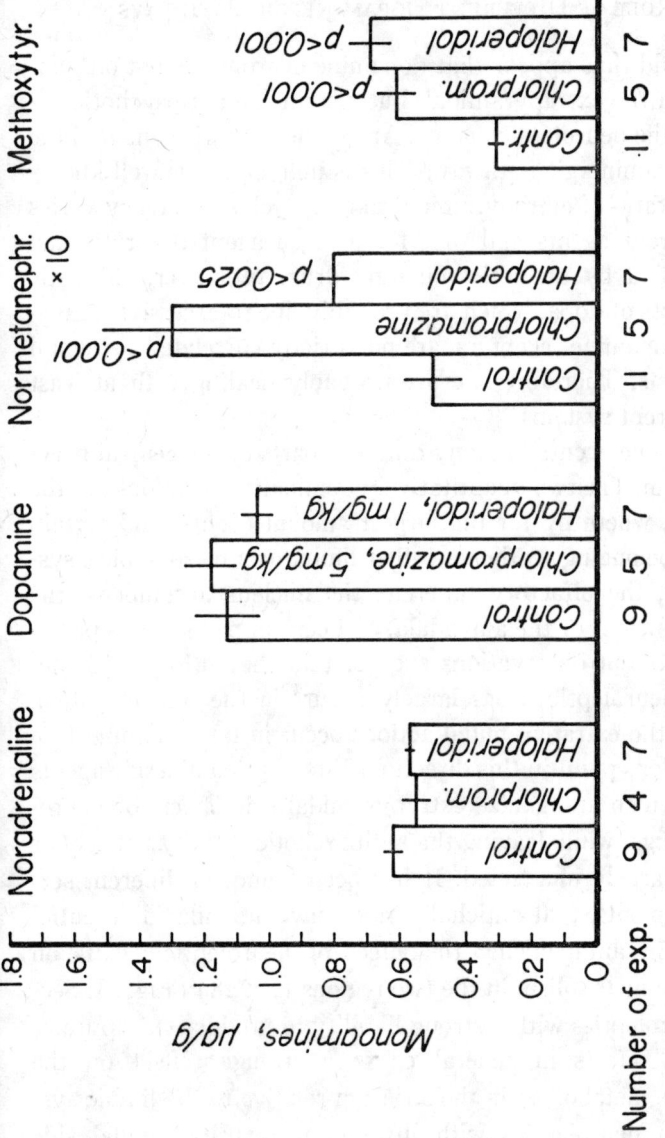

Fig. 1.—Evidence that the Antipsychotic Agents Chlorpromazine and Haloperidol Stimulate the Turnover of Catecholamines in Mouse Brain. (Data compiled from ref. 20, Table 1).

The antipsychotic agents were injected i.p. 1 h after the monoamine oxidase inhibitor nialamide (100 mg/kg) and were killed after another 3 h. Controls received nialamide only.

NOTE: The antipsychotic agents enhanced the accumulation of the 3-0-methylated catecholamine metabolites normetanephrine and 3-methoxy-tyramine but did not influence the levels of noradrenaline or dopamine.

Role of Different Dopaminergic Pathways

It would thus appear that dopamine neurons are not only involved in the extrapyramidal, but also in the antipsychotic actions of the neuroleptic agents. Are we dealing with one and the same dopaminergic pathway? This is unlikely. It is well known that the ratio of extrapyramidal to antipsychotic potency varies for different agents and that for a given agent this ratio can be modified by an anticholinergic drug. Moreover, choreatic side effects of dopa, which are probably due to excessive activation of dopamine receptors, are not strictly correlated to mental side effects. Therefore, we are probably dealing with at least two different systems.

Dopamine occurs in many different parts of the central nervous system. The two quantitatively dominating locations are the striatum, where by far the largest amount occurs, and certain regions belonging to the so-called limbic (or mesolimbic) system, e.g., the olfactory tubercle, the nucleus accumbens, the central nucleus of the amygdala, and certain parts of the paleocortex. Recent observations suggest that the antipsychotic action of neuroleptic drugs largely occurs in the limbic system, whereas the extrapyramidal actions occur in the striatum. Two observations point in this direction. First, anticholinergic agents are known to antagonize extrapyramidal side effects of neuroleptic drugs, while leaving the antipsychotic activity entirely or at least largely unaffected. It has been found, in different sets of experiments, that anticholinergics have a similar differential activity in antagonizing the effect of neuroleptic agents on dopamine metabolism in the two regions (27, 28) (Fig. 2). Second, neuroleptics with a strong liability to produce extrapyramidal side effects in general cause a stronger effect on the dopamine metabolism in the striatum relative to the limbic system than neuroleptics with little or no extrapyramidal side effects (29, 30) (Fig. 3, Table 1).

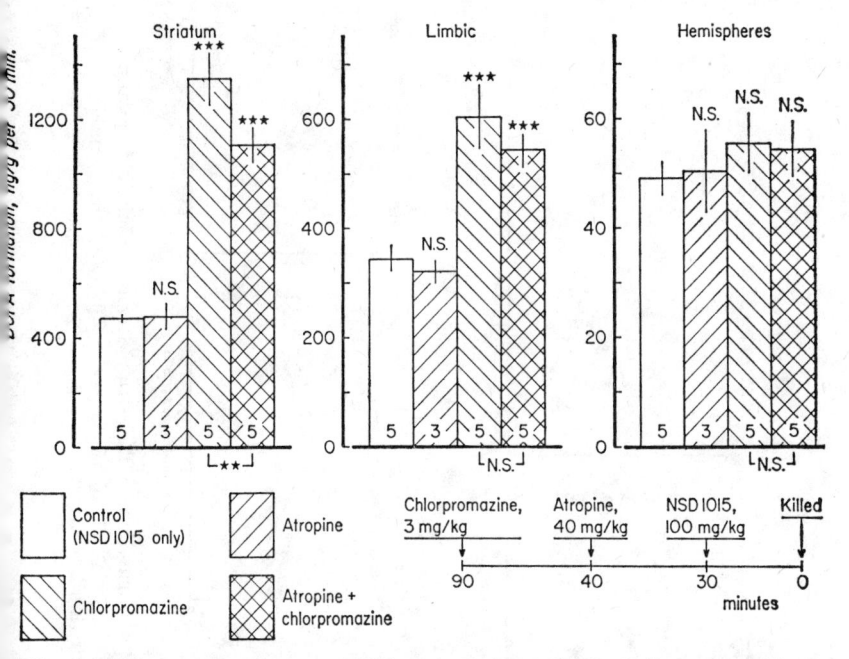

Fig. 2—Effect of Atropine and Chlorpromazine, and Both Drugs Combined, on Dopa Formation in Rat Brain Regions.

All animals received the centrally as well as peripherally active inhibitor of the aromatic amino acid decarboxylase, NSD 1015 (3-hydroxybenzylhydrazine · HCl) i.p. 30 min before death. Injections of chlorpromazine and atropine were given i.p. at time intervals indicated in the Figure. The striatum, limbic dopamine-rich areas and the remaining, predominantly noradrenaline-containing cerebral hemisphere portion were analyzed for dopa.

***$P<0.001$; **$P<0.01$; *$P<0.05$. N.S. $P>0.05$ (comparison with control, if not otherwise indicated).

NOTE: The stimulating action of chlorpromazine on dopa formation was partly counteracted by atropine in the striatum but not, or less so, in the limbic regions. Atropine *per se* did not influence dopa formation.

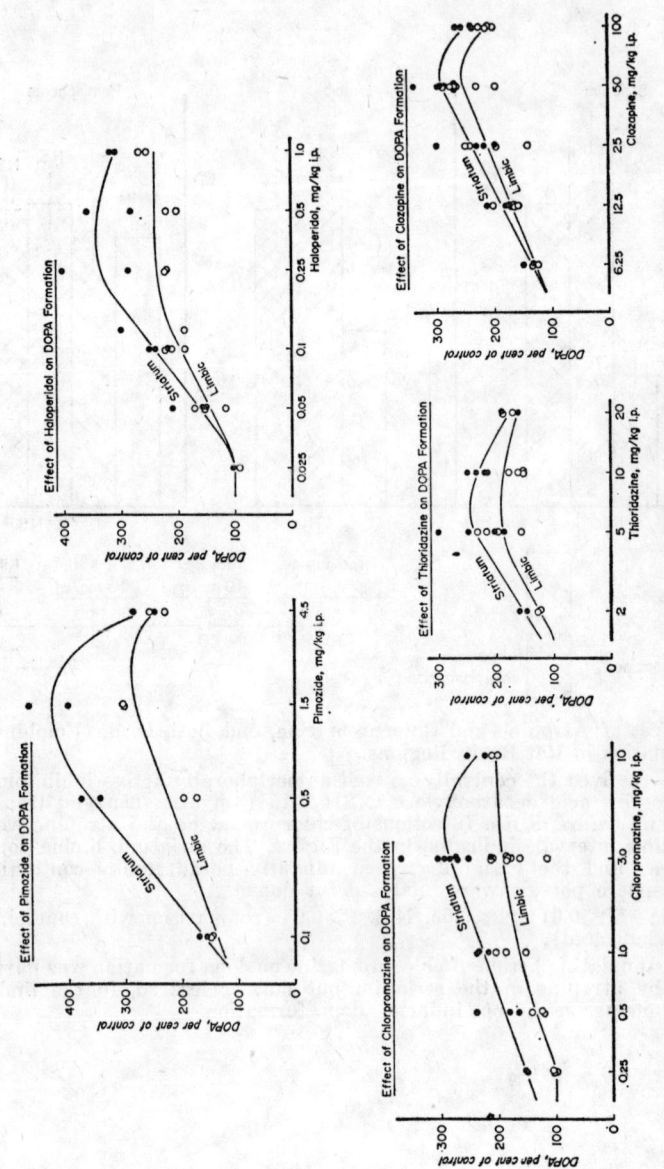

Fig. 3—Effect of Neuroleptics on Dopa Formation in Rat Brain Regions Rich in Dopamine. The neuroleptics were given 60 min before NSD 1015 (100 mg/kg i.p.) and the animals were killed after another 30 min. (Unpublished data of this laboratory.)

Table 1 – Differential Action of Antipsychotic Drugs on DOPA Formation in Striatum vs. Limbic Regions

Drug	Dose, mg/kg	Diff. in % DOPA incr., striatum – limbic	Significance	Extrapyramidal side effects [a]
Pimozide	0.5 – 1.5	153 ± 18.3 (4)		?
Haloperidol	0.25 – 0.5	117 ± 26.1 (4)	$p < 0.025$	1
Chlorpromazine	3	104 ± 11.1 (8)		3
Chlorprom. + Atr.	3	73 ± 9.2 (5)	$p < 0.005$	–
Thioridazine	5 – 10	51 ± 9.3 (8)	$p < 0.05$	4
Clozapine	50 – 100	37 ± 8.8 (10)		5

The differences in % DOPA increase between the striatum and the limbic areas were obtained from the data represented in Fig. 3 and from similar data of an experiment with chlorpromazine and atropine (Atr. 40 mg/kg i.p. 10 min before NSD 1015). The data refer to the doses indicated in the Table. Statistics: t-test.

a) from ref. 39; rank by class; 1 indicates the most side effects.

NOTE: There seems to exist a correlation between a high striatal *vs.* limbic response and liability to extrapyramidal side effects, which may possibly also be inversely related to anticholinergic activity (see ref. 39).

If the antipsychotic action is located in limbic dopaminergic synapses, the question arises as to which of the various dopaminergic regions are involved. This question cannot be answered as yet. Local application of dopamine in the nucleus accumbens has been found to induce hyperkinesia and to stimulate food-reinforced lever pressing, and in the striatum, stereotyped behavior (gnawing, licking, etc.) (31). Further studies are necessary to clarify this point.

ANTIPSYCHOTIC ACTION OF A TYROSINE HYDROXYLASE INHIBITOR

As indicated by the evidence presented above, antipsychotic activity can be induced by interfering with central catecholamines, notably dopamine, in two different ways: a) by blocking the function of the presynaptic storage organelles, leading to neurotransmission failure, and b) by blocking postsynaptic catecholamine receptors. The question then arises of whether inhibition of catecholamine synthesis will alleviate psychotic symptoms.

α-Methyltyrosine is a relatively specific inhibitor of tyrosine hydroylase, the first enzyme involved in catecholamine biosynthesis. This agent has been administered in fairly large doses to psychotic patients, but no antipsychotic action could be detected (32). A possible explanation for this failure could be that the degree of enzyme inhibition was insufficient, clinical dosage being limited by renal toxicity. If insufficient dosage is the explanation, it might be possible to demonstrate an antipsychotic action of α-methyltyrosine by utilizing the ability of receptor-blocking neuroleptics to potentiate the action of this enzyme inhibitor. Such potentiation, of a marked degree, has been demonstrated in animal experiments (33, 34) (Fig. 4).

We have investigated the effect of combined treatment with a phenothiazine and α-methyltyrosine in eight schizophrenic patients with a stationary symptomatology (35-37). In four of these patients, two or three trials have been performed, using a double-blind crossover design in one trial for each patient (37). Before each trial the patient had been treated with a single antipsychotic agent, usually thioridazine, in constant dosage for several months. The trial was started by rating the symptomatology by means of two different rating scales (Fig. 5). Then the dosage of the phenothiazine was slowly reduced stepwise over several weeks, and the ratings were repeated at weekly intervals. After several weeks, when the phenothiazine dosage had been drastically reduced and the care of the patients started to be difficult because of a marked deterioration of the mental condition, α-methyltyrosine was given in a dose which was increased to 2 g daily. This was followed by a certain improvement in a few cases. The dose of phenothiazine was then slowly increased in order to titrate the dose necessary to attain the pre-trial level of ratings. This dose was found to be lower

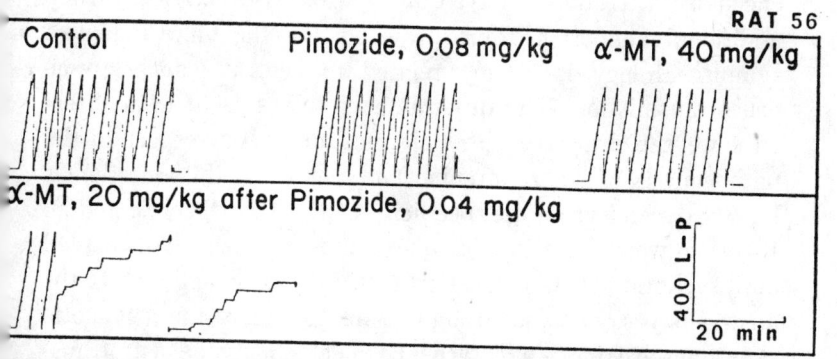

FIG. 4—Potentiation by α-Methyltyrosine of the Pimozide-Induced Inhibition Food-Reinforced Lever Pressing. (Reproduced from ref. 34.)
The cumulative records show that pimozide, 0.08 mg/kg, and α-methyltyrosine (α-MT, H 44/68) 40 mg/kg, when given separately to a rat, have no significant influence on the lever pressing. However, a pronounced inhibition is seen if the two drugs are combined, the doses being only half of those given separately.

than the pre-trial dose in all cases, the average reduction being about 70 percent (range 33 to 98.5 percent). Plasma thioridazine levels were similarly reduced. This combined treatment regimen was maintained for periods varying between 4 weeks and 6 months without any signs of tolerance. During the treatment the concentration of homovanillic acid in the cerebrospinal fluid was reduced by about 80 percent. The treatment period was ended by stopping α-methyltyrosine medication or replacing it by placebo, while keeping the phenothiazine dosage unchanged. In all cases a rapid deterioration of the mental status occurred. The phenothiazine dosage was now increased to the same level as before the trial, and the pre-trial level of symptomatology was reattained.

The Nature of Antipsychotic Drug Effect

Thus, in the presence of a phenothiazine, given in a dosage near the threshold for detectable antipsychotic activity, schizophrenic symptomatology appears to be profoundly influenced by alterations in tyrosine hydroxylase activity. Strong additional support is thus provided for the view that this symptomatology is closely related to central catecholamine neurotransmission. The question then arises as to what inference we can draw from this circumstance with respect to the pathogenesis of schizophrenia. The answer to this question is largely dependent on the specificity of the antipsychotic action. In other words, the crucial question is whether the so-called antipsychotic agents possess true antipsychotic activity. If the answer is yes, we have strong reasons to believe that psychotic symptoms are due to a disturbance in catecholamine neurotransmission or in a functionally closely related mechanism. If on the other hand, the so-called antipsychotic action is only a manifestation of a general depression of mental activity, we are not justified in implicating the catecholamines in the patho-

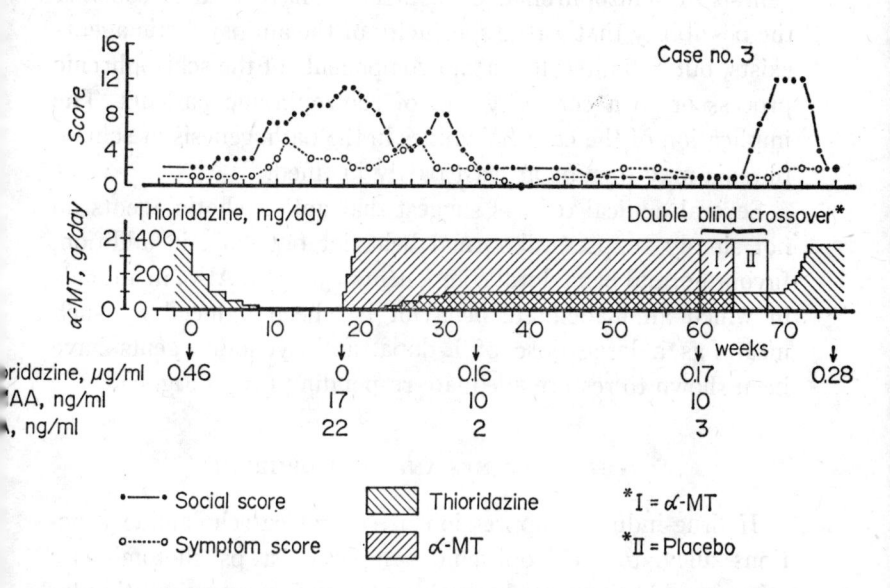

Fig. 5—Potentiation of the Antipsychotic Action of Thioridazine by α-Methyltyrosine (α-MT) in a Schizophrenic Patient. (Data from ref. 37.)

The patient, a 44-year-old male, had suffered from schizophrenia with stationary symptomatology for more than six months. He had been hospitalized and treated with thioridazine ass the only antipsychotic drugs in constant dosage for more than six months. The trial was started by rating the symptoms verbally by a psychiatrist ("symptom score") and behaviorally by the head nurse ("social score"). Then the dosage of thioridazine was reduced stepwise until the care of the patient became difficult. At this time the scores were markedly elevated. α-Methyltyrosine therapy was now started; the dosage being gradually increased to 2 g/day, while keeping the thioridazine dosage at a constant low level. This dose regimen was insufficient to control the condition, and thus the dose of thioridazine was gradually increased until the pretrial symptomatology level was attained. This occurred at a thioridazine dosage of 100 as compared to the pretrial dosage of 375 mg/day. The dose regimen was kept for 30 weeks. During this period the patient tended to be in an even better mental condition than before the trial.

At the termination of the trial α-methyltyrosine was replaced by placebo or α-methyltyrosine, using a double-blind crossover design. During the blind α-methyltyrosine period, which in this case came first, there was no change in the ratings, but during the placebo period a rapid deterioration occurred. The dosage of thioridazine was then gradually increased to the original level, and the symptomatology level was re-attained.

Similar results were obtained in 3 additional schizophrenic patients.

genesis of schizophrenia. Of course, we have to also consider the possibility that a true specificity of the antipsychotic agents exists, but is limited to certain components of the schizophrenic process or to a certain group of schizophrenic patients. The implication of the catecholamines in the pathogenesis of schizophrenia may then be at least partly justified.

Several clinical reports suggest that antipsychotic agents do not simply suppress abnormal behavior but may, in addition, favour normal behavioral components (38, 39). Also, in animals in which an inadequate behavior has been induced by such means as a large dose of L-dopa, antipsychotic agents have been shown to restore adequate responding (40) (Fig. 6).

Amphetamines and Schizophrenia

If drug-induced suppression of central catecholamine functions alleviates schizophrenic symptoms, a psychotomimetic effect would be expected from agents causing excessive stimulation of these functions.

The psychotomimetic agents form a heterogeneous group both from a chemical and pharmacological point of view. Many of them have attracted quite a lot of interest over the years, mainly in view of the possibility that they might provide useful schizophrenia models. The psychotic condition induced by most of these agents can, however, be clearly distinguished from schizophrenia. A striking exception is the amphetamine group of agents, because they are capable of reproducing rather faithfully the picture of paranoid schizophrenia (39). Therefore, the mode of action of amphetamine is of special interest in the present context and, fortunately, it is at least partly understood. It has been shown that amphetamine, even in low dosage, is capable of releasing central (and peripheral) catecholamines and that its central stimulant action is prevented by pretreatment with α-methyltyrosine. The data indicate that ampheta-

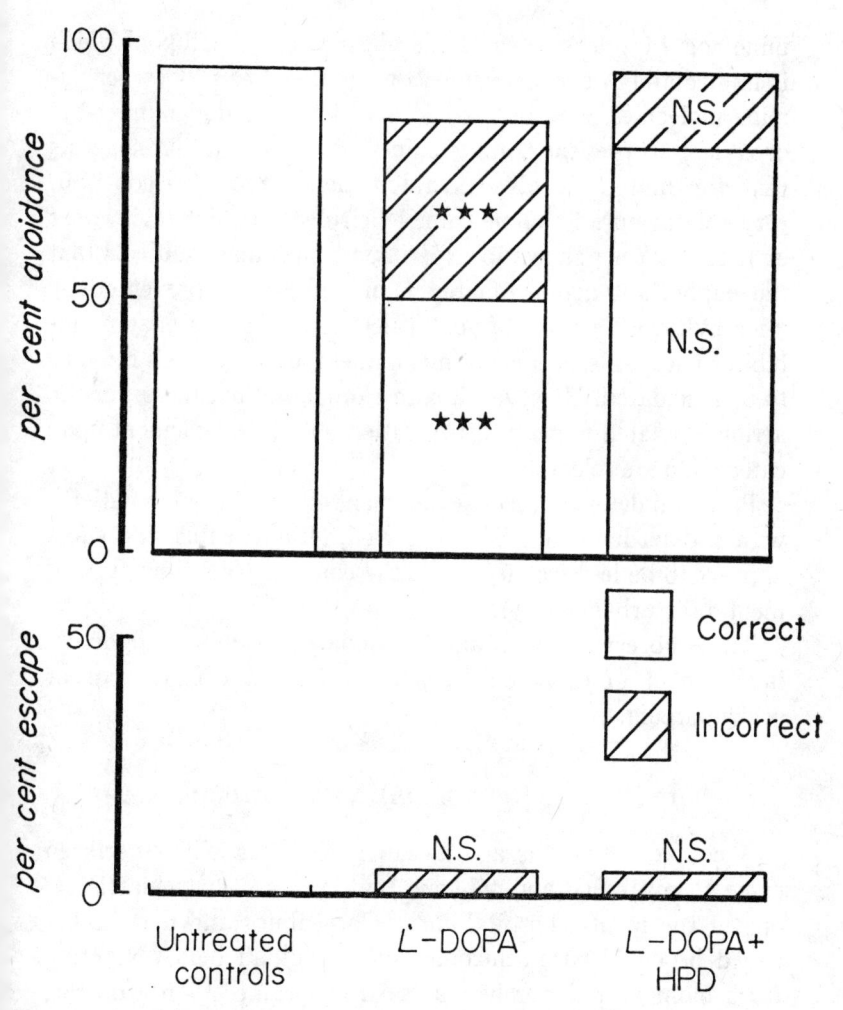

FIG. 6—Loss of Discrimination Ability after Treatment with a Large Dose of L-Dopa and Restoration of Correct Performance by Haloperidol. (Reproduced from ref. 40.)

Rats were trained to pass through one of two passages in a shuttle box. If cue lights above the passage are lit when an auditory warning signal is given the animals were trained to pass through the right passage in order to avoid a grid shock. If the auditory warning stimulus was given without any light signal, avoidance was obtained by passing through the left passage.

NOTE. Untreated animals were trained to almost 100 percent avoidance by using the correct passage exclusively. After treatment with L-dopa, 100 mg/kg i.p. 1 h before the test session together with the inhibitor of the aromatic amino acid decarboxylase, Ro 4-4602 = N^1-(DL-seryl)-N^2-(2,3,4-trihydroxybenzyl) hydrazine HCl, 50 mg/kg i.p., to inhibit the enzyme in peripheral tissues), the animals still reacted to the warning stimulus by passing through one of the openings but no longer discriminated between the correct and the incorrect passage. The addition of haloperidol (HPD), 0.25 mg/kg i.p. 20 min before the test session, restored the performance almost completely to normal.

*** $P<0.001$. N.S. $P>0.05$ (comparisons with untreated controls, Wilcoxon T-test; the values shown are medians, $N = 8$).

mine acts by releasing catecholamines from a small pool which is immediately dependent upon the synthesis of new catecholamine molecules. The failure of an inhibitor of dopamine-β-hydroxylase to prevent amphetamine-induced excitation suggests that dopamine is involved in this action, although a contributory role of noradrenaline cannot be ruled out (for review, see 41). It has been shown in experiments on human subjects that the euphoriant action of amphetamines can be prevented by α-methyltyrosine pretreatment (42). Whether this enzyme inhibitor is capable of preventing amphetamine psychosis remains to be elucidated. However, it seems probable that the psychotic action is related to central stimulation and thus dependent upon catecholamine release.

Paranoid delusions during treatment of Parkinsonian patients with L-dopa have also been reported, although this side effect appears to be less frequent than the confusion-delirium type of mental disturbance (43).

These observations on amphetamine and L-dopa support an involvement of catecholamines in at least a certain type of schizophrenia.

The Possible Role of GABA in Schizophrenia

A couple of months ago a man named Per K. Frederiksen came to my office and told me that he was a psychiatrist in one of the mental hospitals near Gothenburg and that he believed he could cure schizophrenia. I couldn't help wondering for a moment whether he was a patient rather than a doctor, but then he told me about some remarkable preliminary observations. About six weeks earlier he had started to treat schizophrenic patients with baclophen (Lioresal, Ciba: β-(-4-chlorophenyl)-γ-aminobutyric acid), a derivative of GABA capable of penetrating through the blood-brain barrier. The new drug was superimposed on the previous treatment with neuroleptics, which had been only partially successful in these cases. In most of the patients a marked improvement was seen setting in within a few days of baclophen treatment. In particular, the autism and the thought disorder improved with a partial apparent re-integration of the personality. Many of the patients said they could think and read more easily, and they became more communicative. Hallucinations did not disappear, but were less intense and appeared more remote. In some patients psychotic symptoms disappeared altogether. Phenothiazine medication could be reduced or discontinued. In fact, the tolerance to phenothiazines seemed to be reduced by the drug, causing complaints of rigidity, which disappeared after reducing the phenothiazine dosage (44).

The idea that deficiency in GABA may play a role in schizophrenia has been put forward (45, 46). Similar considerations formed the basis of Frederiksen's trial, even though the mode of action of baclophen has not yet been established.

These speculations and observations on the possible role of GABA in schizophrenia are very interesting and will no doubt stimulate basic and clinical research in this area. It may be recalled that an intimate, mutually antagonistic relationship appears to exist between dopamine- and GABA-carrying neuronal pathways, at least in the striatum, and that deficiency of the latter transmitter might well have the same effect as hyperactivity of the former (47-49). It may also be recalled that paranoid delusions and other schizophrenia-like symptoms may occur in Huntington's chorea, in which a deficiency of a striatal GABA pathway has been detected (50, 51). Baclophen has been tried in Huntington's chorea, and some slight improvement was reported (52).

In rats we have observed actions of baclophen on behavior, somewhat similar to those of a neuroleptic agent such as haloperidol (Fig. 7) (53). Thus amphetamine-induced loss of discrimination was restored by baclophen. However, baclophen,

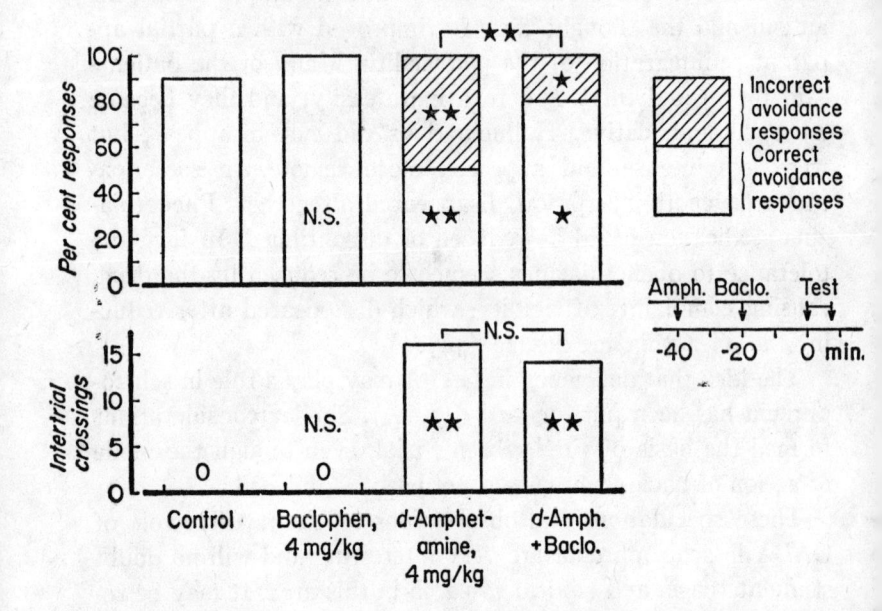

Fig. 7—Loss of Discrimination Ability after Treatment with Dexamphetamine and Restoration of Correct Performance by Baclophen. (Reproduced from ref. 53.)

Rats were trained as described in the legend of Fig. 6.

NOTE: Amphetamine appeared to block the discrimination ability completely, while preserving the responsiveness to the conditioned stimulus. It has acted similarly to L-dopa as shown in Fig. 6. Baclophen restored this ability almost completely, as did haloperidol in the experiment shown in Fig. 6. There are, however, two distinct differences between baclophen and haloperidol: the former drug, unlike the latter, does not antagonize the hypermotility induced by amphetamine, and does not inhibit responding when given alone.

**$p<0.01$, *$p<0.05$, N.S. $p>0.05$, Wilcoxon T-test; the values shown are medians, $N=9$.

unlike haloperidol, did not antagonize amphetamine-induced hypermotility and did not *per se* disrupt conditioned behavior. Thus the profile of baclophen appears to be clearly different from that of classical antipsychotic agents, as assessed both clinically and experimentally. In addition, differences in chemical structure suggest a different point of attack. Future work will decide whether baclophen interacts with GABA or some other neurohumoral transmitter.

REFERENCES

1. CARLSSON, A.: Biochemical and pharmacological aspects of parkinsonism. From Proceedings of the Twentieth Congress of Scandinavian Neurologists, Oslo, 1972. *Acta Neurol. Scandinav.*, 48(Suppl.) 51:11-42, 1972.
2. SHORE, P. A., SILVER, S. L., and BRODIE, B. B.: Interaction of reserpine, serotonin, and lysergic acid diethylamide in brain. *Science*, 122:284-285, 1955.
3. CARLSSON, A. and HILLARP, N. Å.: Release of adrenaline from the adrenal medulla of rabbits produced by reserpine. *Kgl. Fysiogr. Sällsk Lund Förh*, 26: No. 8, 1956.
4. CARLSSON, A., ET AL.: Effect of reserpine on the metabolism of catecholamines. In S. Garattini and V. Ghetti (Eds.): *Psychotropic Drugs*. Amsterdam: Elsevier Publ. Co., 1957, pp. 363-370.
5. CARLSSON, A., LINDQVIST, M., and MAGNUSSON, T.: 3,4-Dihydroxyphenylalanine and 5-hydroxytryptophan as reserpine antagonists. *Nature* (Lond.), 180:1200, 1957.
6. CARLSSON, A., ET AL.: On the presence of 3-hydroxytyramine in brain. *Science*, 127:471, 1958.
7. BERTLER, A. and ROSENGREN, E.: Occurrence and distribution of dopamine in brain and other tissues. *Experientia*, 15:10, 1959.
8. CARLSSON, A.: The occurrence, distribution and physiological role of catecholamines in the nervous system. *Pharmacol. Rev.*, 11: 490-493, 1959.
9. CARLSSON, A., LINDQVIST, M., and MAGNUSSON, T.: On the biochemistry and possible functions of dopamine and noradrenaline in brain. In J. R. Vane, G. E. W. Wolstenholme and M. O'Connor (Eds.): *Ciba Symposium on Adrenergic Mechanisms*. London: J. & A. Churchill, Ltd., 1960, pp. 432-439.
10. EHRINGER, H. and HORNYKIEWICZ, O.: Verteilung von Noradrenalin und Dopamin (3-Hydroxytyramin) im Gehirn des Menschen und ihr Verhalten bei Erkrankungen des Extrapyramidal Systems. *Klin. Wschr.*, 38:1236-1239, 1960.

11. BIRKMAYER, W. and HORNYKIEWICZ, O.: Der L-3,4-Dioxyphenylalanin (=DOPA)-Effekt bei der Parkinson-Akinese. *Wien. Klin. Wschr.*, 73:787-788, 1961.
12. CARLSSON, A., FALCK, B., and HILLARP, N. A.: Cellular localization of brain monoamines. *Acta. Physiol. Scand.*, 56(Suppl.) 196:1-28, 1962.
13. ANDEN, N. E., ET AL.: Demonstration and mapping out of nigro-neostriatal dopamine neurons. *Life Sci.*, 3:523-530, 1964.
14. DAHLSTROM, A. and FUXE, K.: Evidence for the existence of monoamine-containing neurons in the central nervous system. *Acta Physiol. Scand.*, 62 (Suppl.) 232:1-55, 1964.
15. DAHLSTROM, A. and FUXE, K.: Evidence for the existence of monoamine neurons in the central nervous system. *Acta Physiol. Scand.*, 64 (Suppl.) 247:1-85, 1965.
16. FUXE, K. and ANDEN, N. E.: Studies on central monoamine neurons with special reference to the nigro-neostriatal dopamine neuron system. In E. Costa, L. J. Coté, and M. D. Yahr (Eds.): *Biochemistry and Pharmacology of the Basal Ganglia*. New York: Raven Press, 1966, pp. 123-129.
17. ANDEN, N. E., CARLSSON, A., and HAGGENDAL, J.: Adrenergic mechanisms. *Annual Review of Pharmacology*, 9:119-134, 1969.
18. CARLSSON, A.: Drugs which block the storage of 5-hydroxytryptamine and related amines. In V. Erspamer (Ed.): *5-Hydroxytryptamine and Related Indolealkylamines*. Heidelberg: Springer Verlag, 1965, pp. 529-592.
19. CARLSSON, A.: Antipsychotic drugs and catecholamine synapses. *J. Psychiat. Res.*, 11:57-64, 1974.
20. CARLSSON, A. and LINDQVIST, M.: Effect of chlorpromazine or haloperidol on formation of 3-methoxytyramine and normetanephrine in mouse brain. *Acta pharmacol. et toxicol.*, 20:140-144, 1963.
21. AGHAJANIAN, G. K. and BUNNEY, B. S.: Pre- and postsynaptic feedback mechanisms in central dopaminergic neurons. In P. Seeman and G. M. Brown (Eds.): *Frontiers in Neurology and Neuroscience Research 1974*. Toronto: The University of Toronto Press, 1974, pp. 4-11.
22. SEDVALL, G., ET AL.: Mass fragmentometric determination of homovanillic acid in lumbar cerebrospinal fluid of schizophrenic patients during treatment with antipsychotic drugs. *J. Psychiat. Res.*, 11:75-80, 1974.
23. GREENGARD, P.: Molecular studies on the nature of the dopamine receptor in the caudate nucleus of the mammalian brain. In P. Seeman and G. M. Brown (Eds.): *Frontiers in Neurology and Neuroscience Research 1974*. Toronto: The University of Toronto Press, 1974, pp. 12-15.
24. ANDEN, N. E.: Catecholamine receptor mechanisms in vertebrates. In E. Usdin and S. Snyder (Eds.): *Frontiers in Catecholamine Research*. Oxford: Pergamon Press, 1973, pp. 661-665.

25. ANDEN, N. E., ET AL.: Receptor activity and turnover of dopamine and noradrenaline after neuroleptics. *European J. Pharmacol.*, 11:303-314, 1970.
26. NYBACK, H. and SEDVALL, C.: Further studies on the accumulation and disappearance of catecholamines formed from tyrosine-^{14}C in mouse brain. Effect of some phenothiazine analogues. *European J. Pharmacol.*, 10:193-205, 1970.
27. ANDEN, N. E.: Dopamine turnover in the corpus striatum and the limbic system after treatment with neuroleptic and antiacetylcholine drugs. *J. Pharm. Pharmac.*, 24:905-906, 1972.
28. CARLSSON, A.: The effect of neuroleptic drugs on brain catecholamine metabolism. In G. Sedvall, B. Uvnäs, and Y. Zotterman (Eds.): *Antipsychotic Drugs, Pharmacodynamics and Pharmacokinetics*. Pergamon Press, 1975, in press.
29. ANDEN, N. E. and STOCK, G.: Effect of clozapine on the turnover of dopamine in the corpus striatum and in the limbic system. *J. Pharm. Pharmac.*, 25:346-348, 1973.
30. CARLSSON, A.: Receptor-mediated control of dopamine metabolism. In E. Usdin and W. E. Bunney (Eds.): *Pre- and Postsynaptic Receptors*. New York: M. Dekker, Inc., 1975, pp. 49-63.
31. JACKSON, D. M., ANDEN, N. E., and DAHLSTROM, A.: A functional effect of dopamine in the nucleus accumbens and in some other dopamine-rich parts of the rat brain. *Psychopharmacologia* (Berl.), 1975, in press.
32. GERSHON, S., ET AL.: Methyl-p-tyrosine (AMT) in schizophrenia. *Psychopharmacologia*, 11:189-194, 1967.
33. AHLENIUS, S. and ENGEL, J.: Behavioral effects of haloperidol after tyrosine hydroxylase inhibition. *European J. Pharmacol.*, 15:187-192, 1971.
34. AHLENIUS, S. and ENGEL, J.: On the interaction between pimozide and α-methyltyrosine. *J. Pharm. Pharmac.*, 25:172-174, 1973.
35. CARLSSON, A., ET AL.: Potentiation of phenothiazines by α-methyltyrosine in treatment of chronic schizophrenia. *Journal of Neural Transmission*, 33:83-90, 1972.
36. CARLSSON, A., ET AL.: Further studies on the mechanism of antipsychotic action: Potentiation by α-methyltyrosine of thioridazine effects in chronic schizophrenics. *Journal of Neural Transmission*, 34:125-132, 1973.
37. WALINDER, J., ET AL.: Unpublished data, 1974.
38. MAY, P. R. A.: Antipsychotic drugs and other forms of therapy. In D. H. Efron (Ed.): *Psychopharmacology: A Review of Progress 1957-1967*. Washington: U.S. Government Printing Office, 1968, pp. 1155-1176.
39. SNYDER, S. H., ET AL.: Drugs, neurotransmitters, and schizophrenia. *Science*, 184:1243-1253, 1974.
40. AHLENIUS, S. and ENGEL, J.: Antagonism by haloperidol of the L-DOPA-induced disruption of a successive discrimination in the rat. *Journal of Neural Transmission*, 36:43-49, 1975.

41. CARLSSON, A.: Amphetamine and brain catecholamines. In E. Costa and S. Garattini (Eds.): *Amphetamines and Related Compounds. Proceedings of the Mario Negri Institute for Pharmacological Research, Milan, Italy.* New York: Raven Press, 1970, pp. 289-300.
42. JONSSON, L. E., ÄNGGARD, E., and GUNNE, L. M.: Blockade of intravenous amphetamine euphoria in man. *Clin. Pharm. Ther.*, 12:889-896, 1971.
43. GOODWIN, F. K., ET AL.: Levodopa: Alterations in behavior. *Clin. Pharm. Ther.*, 12:383-396, 1971.
44. FREDERIKSEN, P. K.: Preliminärt meddelande angaende Lioresal (Baclofen) vid behandling av schizofreni. *Läkartidningen*, 72: 456-458, 1975.
45. ROBERTS, E.: An hypothesis suggesting that there is a defect in the GABA system in schizophrenia. *Neurosci. Res. Progr. Bull.*, 10:468-480, 1972.
46. STEVENS, J., WILSON, K., and FOOTE, W.: GABA blockade, dopamine and schizophrenia: Experimental studies in the cat. *Psychopharmacologia* (Berl.), 39:105-119, 1974.
47. OKADA, Y., ET AL.: Role of γ-aminobutyric acid (GABA) in the extrapyramidal motor system. 1. Regional distribution of GABA in rabbit, rat, guinea pig and baboon CNS. *Exp. Brain Res.*, 13:514-518, 1971.
48. KIM, J. S., ET AL.: Role of γ-aminobutyric acid (GABA) in the extrapyramidal motor system. 2. Some evidence for the existence of a type of GABA-rich strio-nigral neurons. *Exp. Brain Res.*, 14:95-104, 1971.
49. ANDEN, N. E. and STOCK, G.: Inhibitory effect of gammahydroxybutyric acid and gammaaminobutyric acid on the dopamine cells in the substantia nigra. *Naunyn-Schmiedeberg's Arch. Pharmacol.*, 279:89-92, 1973.
50. PERRY, T. L., HANSEN, S., and KLOSTER, M.: Huntington's chorea. *New Engl. J. Med.*, 288:337-342, 1973.
51. BIRD, E. D., ET AL.: Reduced glutamic-acid-decarboxylase activity of post-mortem brain in Huntington's chorea. *Lancet*, May 19, 1090-1092, 1973.
52. ANDEN, N. E., DALEN, P., and JOHANSSON, B.: Baclofen and lithium in Huntington's chorea. *Lancet*, July 14, 93, 1973.
53. AHLENIUS, S. and ENGEL, J.: Antagonism by baclophen of the d-amphetamine-induced disruption of a successive discrimination in the rat. *Journal of Neural Transmission*, 1975, in press.

7

Synthesis: Biological Contributions to the Theory and Treatment of Schizophrenia

Morris A. Lipton, Ph.D., M.D.

Dr. Klerman has presented a conceptual framework and excellent guidelines for the present day treatment of schizophrenia. He feels that most schizophrenias are best conceptualized as a chronic illness in the medical model, and with acute exacerbations that should be treated vigorously with drugs that interrupt the pathogenic process. Simultaneously the patient should be offered short term hospitalization within a therapeutic milieu. The hospitalization should purposely be kept short to prevent regression and the development of overdependence. After the acute phase has been managed, the patient should be maintained on appropriate psychotropic drugs as needed and he should be restored to his family or to a community setting which is cognitively stimulating but emotionally placid or even tepid. Within the family or community setting psychiatrists may offer the patient what May (1) has called psychotherapeutic management. Such management is fairly concrete, quite directive, educational, and substantive. This type of psychotherapeutic management seems to make a difference in the patient's post-hospital adjustment. Although some interesting experiments are being conducted by Mosher with the treatment of acute schizophrenia psychosocially in a therapeutic community called "Soteria House," on the west coast (2), these have been limited to young, acutely ill schizophrenics. Information assessing the effectiveness of this treatment is not yet available.

In today's state of the art I fully agree with Dr. Klerman's choice of the chronic disease model for most of what we call schizophrenia. It fits most problems which we encounter and it also permits comparison with the strategies and tactics of the internist who deals with chronic diseases like arthritis, diabetes, hypertension and heart failure. In all of these there is no established single etiology. Nonetheless, the internist treats such illnesses regularly while conducting research on many fronts. The results are increasingly better treatment. By contrast the results of psychiatric treatment of schizophrenia have not improved markedly in the past decade. Approximately one-third of our patients will have a single episode with full recovery, another third will have repeated episodes and represent what has become known as the revolving door patient, and the last third seems to disappear into the back alleys or the back wards. On the whole our track record is not very impressive and we must face the question of what we can do to improve it. Clearly there are many reasons why we do not do better. One of them deals with the delivery of health service. Our mental health centers are understaffed, overextended, overcommitted, embroiled in political battles, suffering from lack of public funds and so forth. With persistent efforts we may ultimately be able to do something about these problems. But we have the equally serious problem that there are limits to our understanding and our therapeutic skills even under the best conditions. There is evidence that many patients who have had psychotic breaks do not function optimally. Many retain behavioral and psychological deficits, even if these are not sufficiently great to require rehospitalization. We must therefore attempt to improve the condition of these patients just as internists have done with the chronic illnesses that they treat but do not cure. Following the line of analogy with the problems of the internist, in chronic illness there have been no spectacular breakthroughs and yet the treatment of diabetes is substantially better than it was a decade ago.

There is much more to be learned by comparison of our practices with that of internists. They aspire to cure but often must settle for treatment. We too should aspire to cure and also settle for treatment which will improve the quality of life. Referring back to medicine, for example, the recently developed procedures for coronary bypass surgery seem not to have improved longevity, but by eliminating angina have substantially improved the quality of life. That is a very meaningful contribution, and we should aim for similar types of advances.

What type of thinking and experimentation has permitted the internist to improve his treatment over the years? Two features are readily recognizable. First, internists are not committed to a particular ideology nor a univalent treatment procedure based upon it. Thus, in the treatment of hypertension they may employ low salt diets or diuretics for some patients, while for others they may use low cholesterol diets or resins to lower cholesterol. We would do well in psychiatry to develop a treatment armamentarium that is as versatile as that which the internist is able to employ. Second, they have managed to achieve such versatility largely through diligent, persistent research at all kinds of levels. There is work at the laboratory level designed to understand pathogenesis. Animal models are used to study the production and the treatment of the induced illness. At the clinical level there is constant research activity designed to offer better diagnostic procedures, better subclassification of types of illness and more specific therapies. In most academic centers, clinical training and research are highly integrated. The house officer is expected to conduct some research at either the bench level or the clinical level at some time during his training. From such activity he derives many benefits. He learns how difficult it is to achieve new and reliable information. He becomes a better critic of the literature in his specialty and, most of all, he embarks upon the process of continuing education through the acquisition of the habit of constantly and critically reading the literature.

In this regard I think it's fair to be critical of our own training procedures. Altogether too often, we find our faculties divided into schools of thought and committed to particular ideologies. Such commitments lead us to be method oriented rather than problem oriented. As a consequence the patient may receive only those treatment procedures his physician knows and is comfortable with, when there may be other procedures which might be more effective. Yager (3) has recently written about the dilemmas of obtaining adequate training in psychiatry from the perspective of the resident. What he has said is not less true for the psychiatrist who has finished his residency. There are very few of us who have the conceptual and technical versatility that well trained internists have. In psychiatry very few residents participate in research during their three years of clinical training. The tradition of research as part of the residency program in psychiatry is much weaker than that of the other medical specialties. To compensate for this, the National Institute of Mental Health has funded training for research programs in several training centers. These are open to third year residents as well as 4th and 5th year fellows who wish to have research experience. The results have been generally gratifying insofar as these programs have produced many of our prominent young research people, but they have not been sufficient to establish the tradition of some research experience for every resident. Furthermore, they are in fiscal jeopardy as are so many of the innovative training experiences that have been previously funded by NIMH. Another problem with psychiatry, that I will come back to later, deals with the relevance of basic science and the need for two-way communication between the basic science laboratory and the clinical experiences on the ward and in the community. In medicine, basic sciences of biochemistry, pharmacology, physiology and genetics are considered germane to the clinical experience and virtually every resident acquires some laboratory technology associated with these disciplines. He is thus able not only to interpret basic science data that might be relevant to his clinical problem, but usually he is able to generate such data. Only a small fraction of our psychiatric trainees have this capability.

Granting that schizophrenia is a major public health problem, Dr. Klerman suggests that there is much room for improvement in primary, secondary and tertiary prevention. The previous speakers have addressed themselves to these questions somewhat indirectly, but I shall try to do so more directly.

On the matter of primary prevention, Dr. Cancro summarized the evidence derived from twin studies and adoptive studies that indicates that there is a genetic component to the schizophrenic diathesis. He stated that this evidence does not really offer proof. The question of when strong evidence becomes proof is largely semantic in medicine and biology. Direct proof as we find it in mathematics follows the laws of the syllogism. In medicine we seldom achieve this kind of proof. Instead we continue to gather evidence which increases the probability that our hypothesis is correct. Koch's four postulates for proof that an illness was microbial involved isolation of an organism from the infected animal, growth of the organism in pure culture, the production of the illness by the administration of the cultured organism into a normal animal, and then the re-isolation of the organism from the animal in whom the illness has been induced. Even these postulates do not offer proof in a strictly logical sense. But they make the possibility of error infinitesimally small. They offer overwhelming evidence. The genetic data for schizophrenia become increasingly stronger, and I find them persuasive. Better evidence will come if and when the geneticists are able to link the diathesis for schizophrenia with a polymorphous genetic marker in a one-to-one concordance. This is a problem which is being actively researched, and I suspect that the answer may come within the next few years.

There is a legitimate concern that has been expressed in the discussion groups following some of the speakers about some of the implications of classifying schizophrenia as a genetic illness. May this not be inherently dangerous in terms of public health policy? The answer is that we must be on guard to prevent the misuse of science as applied to public policy, but we must not let our fears stand in the way of our establishing scientific truths. The genetic counseling of families in which there is a history of schizophrenia is a complex and uncertain affair. I've had limited experience with young couples who have themselves not had mental illness but who have a history of mental illness in their families. I have also had some experience with couples in which one of the members has had a psychotic break. I have had no experience with couples in which one of the members is manifestly psychotic when they come for counseling. My policy in general has been to lay out the data as best I can, regarding the risks involved. I begin by pointing out that the risk for schizophrenia is about 1 in 100 for any child; if relatives, but not the parents, have had schizophrenia, I indicate that the chances are less than 1 in 20 that their child will have a psychosis at some time in life. If one of the potential parents has had schizophrenia, I will inform the couple that there may be as high as a 10% chance that their child may have a psychotic break at some point in his life. This is not done in an alarming fashion because I always try to put it into the context of the other illnesses, like diabetes, which also carry some hereditary risk. If there were a problem, like Duchenne dystrophy, I would be discouraging. In schizophrenia I am much less so. I also try to note the quality of the marriage, their economic and social stability, and the nature of the family support system. I never make a firm decision but merely lay out the facts as I see them. In general I tend to include contraceptive advice and information and may suggest delay of pregnancy until the quality and stability of the marriage is well assured. This, as Dr. Klerman noted, is a form of primary prevention.

What other implications might the findings of genetics have for the primary prevention of schizophrenia? Might they lead to earlier recognition of the illness or at least of the diathesis so that one might guess that a particular child will be a greater risk? Population genetics has of course already demonstrated that, statistically, children of parents with schizophrenia are at greater risk, but population genetics offers us nothing of value for the assessment of risk in any individual child. For that we need other techniques which must be derived from biochemistry, neurophysiology or experimental psychology. While we have no well established laboratory tools at present, there are already hints that these are forthcoming. For example, Wyatt and his co-workers have shown that platelet monoamine oxidase may be a genetic marker for the diathesis toward schizophrenia (4). This would be a trait dependent marker as contrasted to a state dependent marker. A trait marker would tell us that the patient is at risk even though he doesn't actually have the illness. A state dependent marker would tell us with a high degree of probability that the illness actually exists and is indeed schizophrenia. Dr. Grinker mentioned in passing that Dr. Phillip Holzman's (5) studies on eye tracking may possibly be a physiological marker of the schizophrenic trait. Dr. Holzman has done relatively simple experiments in which a patient's head is fixed so that he cannot turn it, and a pendulum is then swung in front of him. The patient is asked to track the swinging pendulum with his eyes. Recordings of muscle potential, made by attaching small electrodes near the canthus of the eye, show that normally there is a smooth sinusoidal curve as the eyes go back and forth. Schizophrenics seem to generate a jagged curve. This might be interpreted as a failure to integrate the required patterns needed for tracking. The schizophrenic seems to overreact and then underreact and then overreact again as if he were compensating for the failure to track smoothly. Holzman's data need replication, but if one accepts what he has obtained thus far, this jagged eye-tracking pattern seems to be trait dependent. Schizophrenics in remission show it, schizophrenics on phenothiazines continue to show it, and a large percentage of relatives of schizophrenics show it. I'm informed that Dr. Holzman is about to do a study on monozygotic twins discordant for schizophrenia in Norway, and it will be interesting to see whether his new data will be consistent with his hypothesis.

Another benefit to be derived from study of the genetics of schizophrenia is from the data that show there must be an environmental influence, because even in monozygotic twins the concordance rate for schizophrenia is only 30%-40%. Psychiatrists since the time of Freud have tended to feel that constitution or genetic endowment is immutable. We tend to believe that our job is to help the patient to live well with the traits he has inherited. Drugs are therefore conceptually limited to symptom relief while the real work of treatment goes on in psychotherapy. This position is, of course, wrong. Geneticists have repeatedly demonstrated that expression of a genotype into a phenotype is clearly a function of the environment from the moment of conception. A classic example is phenylketonuria, where a homozygous genotype that would ordinarily go on into mental retardation can be saved if the diet is kept low in phenylalanine during the vulnerable years of the growing brain.

Once the brain has matured, the diet can be normalized to contain the usual quantities of phenylalanine. The patient's blood phenylalanine will be massive, but there will be no mental retardation because the brain was protected during its development. There is thus the full genotype which has been prevented from its behavioral expression as a phenotype.

Another set of examples which I like to use derives from my experience with the A.P.A. Task Force on Megavitamin Therapy. Although there is no evidence to support the thesis that megavitamin therapy is useful in schizophrenia, there is much evidence that there are hereditary vitamin-dependency illnesses which respond to massive doses of vitamins. There are about 20 of these which have been studied by Rosenberg and others (6). They may manifest themselves as anemias, convulsions, mental retardation, athetoid movements, and one case presented as mental retardation and schizophrenia. They always have a demonstrated biochemical abnormality. Such cases follow Mendelian ratios, they occur in young children, and they are dramatically responsive to the appropriate water-soluble vitamin in doses of twenty to several hundred times the usual requirement. When such doses are given, the genotype does not express itself phenotypically. The point here is that while the genes cannot yet be changed, their expression can be by an appropriate environment.

This brings us to the nature of the environment which might be protective. Unfortunately we know little of this, but do recognize that it may involve the physical, chemical nature of the intrauterine environment, the birth process itself, and almost certainly the interaction of the infant and young child with its mother and other members of the family. These have been studied, as Dr. Chodoff has pointed out, and some aberrant patterns of family communication have emerged. Unfortunately, we cannot yet adequately describe the nature of the interpersonal environment that would either protect a child or predispose him to schizophrenia. In fact, one might seriously question, as did one of the speakers, whether a universal environment guaranteed to protect or generate illness in a child can exist. There is so much variance in the needs of children that what might be ideal for one might be a disaster for another.

We may be able to generate some useful hypotheses by playing a game. I have done this for years. Suppose, for example, you had a Hitlerian mandate to produce schizophrenia in virtually 100% of a population under study, without ethical restraints. How would you produce it? This type of game has two advantages. First, if one could create this environment in fantasy, the odds are that somewhere in the world one might actually find it. Second, if one could define the pathogenic psychological environment, one might be able to eliminate the psychotoxic elements and thus have a preventive one.

The first thing to do, I suppose, would be to breed schizophrenics. This would offer a degree of vulnerability that would produce schizophrenia 30%-40% of the time. But this is not enough for the experiment. What else might be added on? I've thought about this for a long time. Clearly I don't know the answer, but the environment I'd work with first would be one whose primary characteristic was unpredictability. I suspect that most of you would agree that few stresses for man can match that of uncertainty. We are all personally familiar with the stress in the form of questions like: Will there be a war in the Middle East? What is the future of our profession? What kind of world will our children live in? Imagine the stress of the child who is unable to predict parental behavior, and who does not know whether a given need will be recognized and gratified, nor whether a given act, which once received a reward, would be now rewarded, punished or ignored. Ideally the environmental stress should interact with the genetic diathesis in order to be maximally effective. That is, if there were some central nervous system inconstancy in the susceptible individual, it might resonate with the environmental inconsistency to produce a situation where reliable interpersonal relationships might be impossible, and hypervigilance or withdrawal into autism and anhedonia might be a reasonable defensive maneuver. To the individual it need not matter whether the environment was actually unreliable or whether he perceived it that way because of his own defects. But if both were unreliable, the effects might be interactive.

Are there data to support or deny the possibility of exceptional unreliability built into the schizophrenic organism? Holzman's eye tracking finding in schizophrenics might be associated with perceptual inconsistency for that individual. The particular vigilance of paranoid schizophrenia and the apparent inability of the schizophrenic to filter out inappropriate stimuli from appropriate ones could also lead to the perception of a highly unreliable world even if the world were itself reliable.

If inconstancy and unreliability were the hallmark of the schizophrenic environment, in what kind of family might it exist? It need not be a family in which one or more of the parents is schizophrenic. There may well be families which, like the old story of some executives, "give ulcers but don't get them." This is a point to keep in mind when examining the implications of the European studies in which children with no genetic evidence of a tendency toward schizophrenia are adopted into families in which one or more parents develops schizophrenia. Such studies, while thus far incomplete, seem to show that the biologically unsusceptible child is not prone to develop schizophrenia. Even if this should prove to be the case, it still does not follow that schizophrenia cannot be culturally transmitted.

If there are psychosocial environments which are schizophrenogenic, then there must be some which are protective; and if these can be defined they will be of great value in primary and secondary prevention. But we know little about them. May (1) has demonstrated that psychoanalytic psychotherapy offered four times a week to patients in state hospitals offers no significant advantage over conventional treatments, while drugs offer a distinct advantage. But he has also pointed out the advantages of psychotherapeutic management along with drugs in outpatient care. There is a tendency to forget that there are many forms of psychological treatment other than insight oriented or psychoanalytic psychotherapy. Some of these may have considerable utility. Thus, as Dr. Klerman told us, he and his co-workers have found that in the post-hospital adjustment of depressed patients, antidepressants significantly diminish relapse and improve work performance. But drugs do nothing for interpersonal relationships, and once-a-week psychotherapy with social workers improves these relationships. Drugs and psychotherapy are therefore additive. Hogarty, as Dr. Klerman mentioned, has shown that once-monthly contact with a social worker has beneficial effects for the schizophrenic maintained in the community on drugs. Much more research on the interaction of drugs and varied psychological treatments is needed. Such studies should be rigorous in design and should include effects on personal and family dynamics.

Another issue from the genetic and clinical data which warrants mention deals with the question of how many schizophrenias there are. Here again there seems to be a tendency to polarize without adequate data. Some feel that there is a single schizophrenia, others that there may be a very large number. In considering this we may again take recourse to the medical model. There are only a few types of diabetes and hypertension; and even the types of mental retardation can be classified as genetic, brain injured, metabolic, nutritional and psychosocial. A similar type of classification might be made for schizophrenia. In passing I should say that I have no problem in accommodating a purely psychosocial concept of schizophrenia. Nature is full of phenocopies that resemble genetic phenotypes but which lack the defective gene. If retardation can be produced psychosocially, why not schizophrenia? But if this is the case, it is worth examining a bit more closely. Psychosocial retardation has serious consequences for the individual and for society, but it seldom leads to the profound retardation associated with biological causes. Psychosocial schizophrenia similarly will probably prove to be less severe than that which involves the genetic trait. Comparison of schizophrenia with mental retardation may be useful in still another regard. We have learned from the study of retarded children and animals that there are critical periods when the central nervous system is appropriately plastic for learning. If these periods are passed without exposure to the appropriate stimuli for learning, irreversible behavioral deficits may result. Critical periods for learning vary tremendously in duration. Animal experiments suggest that some, like sexual behavior, are determined in the first few days of life. Others, like learning a new language without an accent, may not occur until puberty. From research related to child development we will learn more about critical periods and also about the possibilities for reversibility of behavioral deficits, engendered early in life, during later life.

There is a continuing argument about the number of genes involved in schizophrenia. Some advocate a single gene, some several genes. I am not qualified to discuss this matter but should point out that even advocates of the polygenic theory limit the number of possible genes to a small number. Winokur (7), for example, feels that there may be a powerful gene for paranoid schizophrenia and a weaker one for hebephrenia. If both are present, there may result a hebephrenic patient with paranoid qualities. On the other hand, if the paranoid gene alone is present there may be paranoid schizophrenia. This suggests that there may be at least two genetic forms of schizophrenia. I rather like this concept because it fits something that Dr. Mandell discusses. There is general acceptance of the finding that the psychosis resulting from amphetamine is clinically indistinguishable from paranoid schizophrenia. But why is it always paranoid schizophrenia? Why is it never simple schizophrenia nor hebephrenic schizophrenia? We do not have the answer to this question, but it at least suggests that paranoid schizophrenia may be a different entity from the other schizophrenias. From what we know of the pharmacology of amphetamine, from animal studies, we would expect it to cause hyperdopaminergic reactions with increased vigilance and stereotypy. The clinical paranoid schizophrenic has similar behavioral features, and we may assume that he too is in a hyperdopaminergic state. Since all known antipsychotic agents have the property of blocking dopamine receptors, we have a rationale for the treatment of paranoid schizophrenia. But our rationale for the effectiveness of these drugs is much weaker for the withdrawn, simple or hebephrenic schizophrenias.

Wise and Stein (8) have suggested that a fundamental weakness of the schizophrenic may be a deficiency in his midbrain reward system. Such a deficiency could lead to an inability to reinforce behavior through reward. This in turn could lead to withdrawn or asocial behavior. The reward system of animals has been shown to involve norepinephrine as a neurotransmitter. When norepinephrine is experimentally depleted, electrical self-stimulation of the brain by rats diminishes markedly. Although it is not possible to directly measure the reward system of man, it can be approached indirectly. Stein, knowing that the last enzyme involved in the biosynthesis of noradrenaline (from dopamine) is dopamine-β-hydroxylase (DBH), measured the DBH content of brains from schizophrenics obtained at autopsy. He found it to be low in accord with the prediction from his hypothesis. However, very recently, Wyatt et al. failed to replicate these results (9). Wise and Stein (10), in commenting on Wyatt's results, pointed out that if Wyatt's patients were divided into paranoids and non-paranoids, the brain DBH levels from the non-paranoids would be low, confirming their data, while that of the paranoids would be within normal range. Perhaps they are correct in separating these two forms of schizophrenia as the data with amphetamine and Winokur's genetic data would suggest.

Despite the clinical advances which have followed the introduction of psychotropic drugs and their value in generating new hypotheses, we are left with some puzzling questions. Why, for example, do our drugs take so long to act? Referring back to internal medicine as a reference point: a heart can be digitalized, or a blood stream sterilized with an antibiotic in a few days. Psychotropic drugs, by contrast, take weeks to act therapeutically. Yet their side effects occur as quickly as most drugs act. How can we explain this? One explanation is that we have poor and primitive drugs and that we will someday get better and faster ones. On the other hand, the slow action of the drugs may be trying to tell us something about the nature of the illness. The usual models of illness we employ tend to be toxic or deficiency models, and we expect to obtain quick restitution of function. But suppose the "psychic wounds" or "psychic injuries," of which we've talked for years, turn out to be more than metaphors. Perhaps there really are wounds which take time to heal as does a burn or a damaged liver. The time course of recovery from such injuries corresponds much more closely to the course of recovery from a schizophrenic break. Protein synthesis, which is slow, is required for recovery from tissue injury. Perhaps it is also required for recovery from a psychosis.

This presents us with a semantic problem. On the one hand we describe schizophrenia as a functional psychosis because we have never been able to find clear somatic pathology in the brain or elsewhere. And yet I have suggested that psychic breaks, wounds or injuries may be real. This apparent contradiction can be resolved if we recognize that the demonstration of organic pathologies is limited by our instrumentation. If an optical microscope cannot see it, perhaps an electron microscope would. Perhaps it can be noted only by chemical tests which can detect metabolic lesions which have no visible anatomical correlates. An example which comes to mind is that of the convulsive state produced by thiamine deficiency. This is commonly called a functional lesion because there are no associated anatomical findings; yet chemical analysis reveals a huge excess of pyruvic acid and grossly disordered carbohydrate metabolism.

If indeed it should turn out to be the case that the major psychoses have associated chemical derangements, then appreciable time might be required for their correction; and drugs might be required for prolonged periods while repair of the disturbances takes place. In the early studies of the biochemical pharmacology of psychotropic drugs there was a strategic error made in describing their mode of action in terms of their acute effects on animals; yet clinically the drugs are given chronically. It has turned out that the changes brought about by chronic drug use differ considerably from those noted acutely. For example, most of the norepinephrine released by a presynaptic neuron is ordinarily inactivated by reuptake into the neuron which released it. In acute experiments imipramine inhibits this reuptake inactivation. In chronic experiments much of the effect of imipramine is lost. Yet imipramine as a therapeutic agent is useful only when given chronically.

Dr. Mandell describes biochemical changes associated with chronic drug administration. He refers to a recent experiment by Post which is still unpublished. In a patient given probenecid, which prevents the exit of acid metabolites through the blood brain barrier, the level of homovanillic acid (HVA) reflects the rate of turnover of dopamine, its parent compound. HVA levels in psychotic patients are not especially high. But if the patient is given chlorpromazine for three weeks, it is elevated about 3 fold. At three weeks most patients are not clinically improved in a major way. If the chlorpromazine is continued for another three weeks, the patients are usually in clinical remission. At this time the HVA levels have returned to the pretreatment level. It appears as if the chlorpromazine perturbs the system, initiating a series of changes which may begin by altering the rate of dopamine turnover. But when the drug is continually administered until the patient is in clinical remission, secondary homeostatic adjustments take place which result in lowering the dopamine turnover. The secondary changes which occur may be more important for clinical remission than those initiated by the chlorpromazine. What these secondary changes are we do not yet know. Receptor sensitivity may change, enzyme induction may lead to alterations in the metabolic rate of other biogenic amines or even of amino acid transmitters. There is reason to believe that not only one transmitter is disordered in the mental illnesses, but that the balance between multiple systems is upset.

Dr. Carlsson discusses a Swedish co-worker who has taken patients who responded poorly to phenothiazines and given them a gamma amino butyric acid derivative. Such patients apparently improve substantially and even require less phenothiazine. Since gamma amino butyric acid is known to be an inhibitory neurotransmitter, these results suggest that there is an imbalance between excitatory and inhibitory systems in schizophrenia. A similar imbalance between dopaminergic and cholinergic systems seems to exist in Parkinson's disease, and it is likely that similar imbalances exist in other CNS illnesses. Perhaps it is the restoration of an appropriate balance which requires a long time.

Finally, let us consider animal models briefly. It is quite evident from the medical literature that when an appropriate animal model is generated progress is rapidly made. Yet psychiatrists have used animal models very little in research, particularly in the major mental illnesses. We have almost taken the position of implying that schizophrenia is a disease of the soul and since only man has a soul there is no point to looking at lower species. Yet we know, since Darwin, that animals have emotions and express them. Probably they cannot express them in all the subtle forms that a human can, and we still have much to learn about how to understand them, but clearly the emotions are there. Since they are there, emotional disorders are also there and can be studied profitably, as the following examples will show.

Dr. McKinney's studies on monkeys, at Wisconsin, involve the induction of severe psychopathological states by psychosocial manipulation (11). He has shown that monkeys that are reared in isolation in vertical chambers come to have many features that one might call psychotic, autistic or depressed. He is able to treat that condition with phenothiazines or psychologically with what he calls monkey therapists. These are baby monkeys whose needs for contact make them interact with the sick monkeys in a fashion which is therapeutic. McKinney has nicely demonstrated that psychopathology induced psychogenically can respond either to psychological treatment or to phenothiazine treatment. He has not yet done experiments involving both treatments simultaneously.

Corson's work with dogs, at Ohio State, is also relevant (12). He has a model that he believes resembles hyperkinesis. By random selection, he finds dogs that cannot be conditioned. They won't tolerate a Pavlovian harness but tear it up. Whether such dogs result from genetic or experimental influence is not known. Such dogs do not respond to chlorpromazine; but they do very well on amphetamine. When they are on amphetamine they can be conditioned. Moreover, the conditioning in turn is not drug dependent. Once they've been conditioned, amphetamine can be withdrawn and they stay conditioned. This is an interesting example of the interaction of pharmacotherapy and conditioning psychotherapy. Corson obtains similar results with vicious dogs, dogs that have been brought to him when the alternative is destruction. How they got that way he's not at all sure, except that a lot of them have a little bit of cocker spaniel in them. Perhaps this breed has a genetic diathesis. Beyond that, they have usually been mistreated. They are really vicious; food must be thrown to them as one doesn't dare go near them. If they are given amphetamines they become docile and can be petted. When one pets them they become socialized. After a while, one can withdraw the amphetamines and they stay as nice pets. This is again an animal model of interaction of a type of social therapy, or psychological therapy, with drug therapy. I think we could use these models. This type of thinking and experimentation might help us to begin to better integrate the phenomena of psychotherapy with (rather than versus) pharmacotherapy.

Future research in biological psychiatry has two large needs. One is obviously money. It is appalling that the average state in the U.S. spends 0.3% of its total mental health budget on research and 99.7% on services. In addition, the time is past when there were plenty of federal funds. This is especially pitiful at a time when there are emerging conceptual breakthroughs. We are creating a social climate in which young people are not eager to get into these significant professional areas. It is too risky for them, and we are unable to train the right kinds of people.

We have one other great need. That great need is for top people in the field. We need more people like Roy Grinker and others of his stature. Dr. Grinker has invested close to 50 years of research in psychiatry. As he so nicely puts it, he stayed on the ground rather than in airplanes, and tended his shop. He has been enormously flexible in changing his point of view, yet he is not whimsical. At an age substantially beyond most people's retirement he is embarking on new research, with Phil

Holzman and others, that is projected over the next two decades. We need a lot more of this dedicated scholarship and research.

REFERENCES

1. MAY, P. R.: *Treatment of Schizophrenia.* New York: Science House, 1968.
2. MOSHER, L. R., MENN, A. L., and MATTHEWS, S. M.: Soteria: A new treatment for schizophrenia—one year follow-up data. Read before the 51st Annual Meeting of the American Orthopsychiatric Association, San Francisco, April 1974.
3. YAGER, J.: A survival guide for psychiatric residents. *Archives of General Psychiatry*, 30:494, 1974.
4. WYATT, R. J., MURPHY, D. L., BELMAKER, R., COHEN, S., DONNELLY, C. H., and POLLIN, W.: Reduced monoamine oxidase activity in platelets: A possible genetic marker for vulnerability to schizophrenia. *Science*, 179:916, 1973.
5. HOLZMAN, P. S., PROCTOR, L. R., LEVY, D. L., YASILLO, N. J., MELTZER, H. Y., and HURT, S. W.: Eye-tracking dysfunctions in schizophrenic patients and their relatives. *Archives of General Psychiatry*, 31:143, 1974.
6. ROSENBERG, L. E.: Vitamin-dependent genetic disease. *Hospital Practice*, 5:59-66, 1970.
7. WINOKUR, G., MORRISON, J., CLANCY, J., and CROWE, R.: Iowa 500: The clinical and genetic distinction of hebephrenic and paranoid schizophrenia. *Journal of Nervous and Mental Disease*, 159:12-19, 1974.
8. WISE, C. D. and STEIN, L.: Dopamine-β-hydroxylase deficits in the brains of schizophrenic patients. *Science*, 181:344, 1973.
9. WYATT, R. J., SCHWARTZ, M. A., ERDELYI, E., and BARCHAS, J. D.: Dopamine-β-hydroxylase activity in brains of chronic schizophrenic patients. *Science*, 187:368, 1975.
10. WISE, C. D. and STEIN, L.: Comment. *Science*, 187:370, 1975.
11. MCKINNEY, W. T., YOUNG, L. D., SUOMI, S. J., and DAVIS, J. M.: Chlorpromazine treatment of disturbed monkeys. *Archives of General Psychiatry*, 29:490, 1973.
12. CORSON, S. A.: The violent society and its relation to psychopathology in children and adolescents. *Society, Stress and Disease*, Vol. 2. Lennart Levi (Ed.). Oxford University Press (in press).